Mark,

Take On Visions & Real

Roety

The Jesus System

G-12
Groups of Twelve

The Jesus System

G-12

Groups of Twelve

*Launching your Ministry
into Explosive Growth*

ROCKY J. MALLOY

The Jesus System Groups of Twelve
Launching Your Ministry Into Explosive Growth
Rocky J. Malloy

ISBN 1-930941-31-5
Copyright © 2002 Rocky J. Malloy
Shield of Faith Ministries
P.O. Box 327
Texas City, Texas 77590

Editorial Consultants: Cynthia Hansen, Denise Whiteurst
Cover Design and Layout: Cristina Fernández, Impact Productions
Text Design: Cristina Fernández, Impact Productions

Table of Contents

Foreword   9

Preface   11

Introduction: Key To Understanding the System   17

Chapter 1: The Vision   23

Chapter 2: Win   31

Chapter 3: Consolidate   51

Chapter 4: Disciple   75

Chapter 5: Send   91

Chapter 6: A Timeline of Success   95

Chapter 7: The History of Cells   109

Chapter 8: Why Cells?   125

Chapter 9: Why Some Say Cells Don't Work   139

Chapter 10: How the G-12 Structure Works   147

Chapter 11: Ministry Networks   191

Chapter 12: Implementing the Vision   199

Chapter 13: How To Conduct a Successful Cell Meeting   227

Chapter 14: Group Dynamics   255

Dedication

To pastors,
missionaries, and
traveling ministers
around the world
desiring a better way
to serve God and man.

Acknowledgments

This book would not be complete without special thanks to some very special people.

First, I would like to thank my wonderful wife, Joske. In between caring for our four children (two of whom she is home-schooling) plus all the demands of full-time ministry, she still managed to find the time to assist with the original drafts and with typing and editing while continuing to encourage and inspire me.

Second, I would like to thank my friends, Tom Shelby, Jerry Popenhagen, Kyle Dickson, Bobby Gass, and Steve Hardwick — all of whom encouraged and motivated me to finish the book in a timely fashion.

Also, I would like to thank Mary Allen and William Babcock for assisting with the edit of the original text. Their talents went a long way in making this book well organized and easy to understand.

And finally, I would like to thank Tom Newman, Mitch Putnam and David Copeland for making the book come to life.

Foreword

All over the world, churches are looking for answers to the needs of people. But Jesus is still the answer! He alone can fulfill and satisfy the human heart.

Yet how do we communicate the life of Jesus? What can we do to help people understand His Word and receive His Spirit? I believe "cells" — small groups within a local body of believers — are a key to touching people at the depths of their being. Small groups provide an opportunity for people to build relationships and release ministry. These groups provide a unique setting for worship, prayer, teaching, fellowship, and evangelism.

Rocky Malloy has experienced a special touch of God's grace in his life. His vision to impact the nation of Bolivia has been expanded by the "G-12" model for cells. His concepts and ideas will give you inspiration for your own small groups.

Jesus is in the process of building His Church. To play an effective role in His end-time plan, you must get yourselves in position to work with Him. This book can help you!

Billy Joe Daugherty
PASTOR VICTORY CHRISTIAN CENTER
TULSA, OKLAHOMA

AUTHOR'S NOTE: Billy Joe Daugherty pastors one of the most successful cell churches in the United States. His church uses the G-12 cell system.

Preface

To the surprise of some, one of the greatest reasons to support missions is the benefit received back home. You see, missionary efforts don't just reap a harvest overseas. Although many have thought of missions as a dead-end, one-way street, that isn't so. Sowing and reaping is a well-established Bible principle (Gen. 8:22). Every time we sow into another culture, we reap many benefits and blessings, one of which is a greater understanding of who Christ is and who we are in Him.

The earliest model of Christianity (as described in the opening chapters of the Book of Acts) is a Jewish one. The earliest Christians understood the significance of Jesus in essentially Jewish terms. They were all Jews by birth and inheritance, so everything about Jesus made sense to them in terms of Jewish history and Jewish destiny. Jesus' own brother became known as James the Just, or James the Righteous — a title that in the Jewish sense refers to the fulfillment of the Law.

What reason had early Christians to abandon the Torah or the Law? Jesus Himself said He did not aim to destroy it; He would not sanction the loss of a single jot or tittle of God's Law (Matt. 5:18). So attached were those early believers to the temple that they seem to have made it their regular meeting place and the temple liturgy, the staple of their worship.

Above all, Jesus was the national Savior of Israel; the One who would redeem the nation and make the significance of redemption clear to the nations. Thus, for the early Jewish Christians, Jesus was a Jewish Savior whose work could not be fully understood without reference to the nation of Israel.

I said all that to say this: We are not much different than those early Christians were in regard to religiosity. We think, *Who* could know more than the American Christian? *Ninety-five percent of all known Christian works are in English!* We sound much like those early Jewish believers, among whom the attitude prevailed: *Who could know Jesus better than we do?* That attitude, however, was inherently flawed, for it restricted man's understanding of Jesus to one culture and one people.

As Christ was taken into the Greek world, it posed questions for the early Jewish Christian that did not naturally arise in the Jewish world where Christianity originated. With each answer to these new questions, Jesus became greater, grander, and more complex in His relations with humanity than the earliest Jewish concepts of the Messiah could convey.

In reality, the stature of Christ increases as each fresh new culture is incorporated into the Church, which is His Body. This is why the local church back home grows in Christ as the congregation expands its missions efforts.

The transporting of Christianity into a Greek setting required the translation of central Christian doctrines into Greek. This in turn raised Greek questions about Christ that required Greek answers. Similarly, the subsequent transporting of the Christian faith into a European setting raised questions about Christ relating to the laws and customs of Western societies.

For instance, Western European Christians demonstrated more interest in the doctrine of the Atonement than early Christian writers had thought necessary. The doctrine of Atonement that resulted from Western European interest helped open up a new area of understanding to the entire Body of Christ regarding the significance of Christ's work of redemption.

The difference between the Christian world of the last century and that of our day is that the majority of Christians are now

Africans, Asians, Latin Americans, and Pacific Islanders — and the proportion is increasing daily. Christianity is now primarily a non-Western religion and, by all present indications, will steadily become even more so. In other words, missionaries are getting the job done. The cell concepts coming from Asia and now from South America reflect their pre-Christian cultural processes. As these cultures have absorbed Christ, their contribution has helped awaken the Church.

Not many of us would throw out our toilets because they originated in China or drive on steel hubs because rubber first came from South America. Why then would we be too proud to receive revelations of Christ from the same continents? Consider the tabernacle of the "Jewish God." Although the vessels and the tabernacle hangings were divinely directed in the making, they consisted of Egyptian gold and Egyptian cloth.

The first "Jesus community" was a Messianic one. To become a convert involved not just a change of heart but also a change of direction. In other words, "conversion" included the meaning of *turning what was already there in a new direction*. It was not a matter of substituting something new for something old. That would be proselytizing, a method the early Church could have adopted but deliberately chose not to. Nor was conversion a matter of adding something new to something old; that would be redundant. Rather, Christian conversion involved a process of redirection.

NOTE: This "redirection" process of conversion is separate from the recreative process that goes on in the spirit of man at conversion, when the resurrection of the human spirit takes place and a new, living spirit replaces the former, spiritually dead spirit (2 Cor. 5:17).

Jesus transformed Jewish culture through the Gospel but did not destroy the continuity of the Jewish life in the process. On the contrary, He produced a model of thought and life that was "Christian" because He was at its center yet that remained essentially Jewish.

However, when the same Christian principles were applied to Greek believers, a whole range of awkward questions arose about social customs. The conversion of Greeks opened up their social and family life to the influence of Jesus Christ. It forced them to think of the implications of their daily life and their social identity being integrally tied to Christ.

This was a risky process, with many areas of doubt and difficulty. However, risk, tension, and controversy are essential to the process of conversion. As disturbing and challenging as this process was for the Greek Christians, it was also vital to their spiritual survival. In the end, it forever altered that society's social customs of life, *but it did so from the inside out.*

The "G-12 cell system" that originated in South America is a case in point. (NOTE: "G-12" stands for "Group of 12," as will be explained in later chapters.) It is a wonderful example of a culture other than our own attaining the "fullness of Christ" through the power of the Gospel. It is also a good example of the way the Gospel is expanded when pagans come into the community of faith — not merely expanded into new languages but into the deeper thoughts of an alien culture.

This is a new direction that must develop from the inside out. However, managing the revival that this new direction brings can be quite a challenge. I know this from personal experience!

We find ourselves in a special time — in a new reality where the ever-increasing majority of the global Christian community is made up of non-Western peoples. Language is but the outer shell of a much more fundamental diversity of thoughts and practices into which the Christian message must be translated. I feel very fortunate to be a bridge between what is happening on the mission field and what is going on in the Western world.

I am totally convinced that the G-12 cell system is the solution to the challenges of the Church in the new millennium as it was in the first century. It successfully crosses all cultural barriers because it is a "Jesus thing." It is how He introduced Heaven into earth's culture. The question is, how much can we learn from Jesus' example?

Working with the cell system that Jesus gave us greatly facilitates both personal and corporate growth. For one thing, the problems inherent with governing any group become restricted to small factions, thus protecting the group at large. Cell groups act like compartments in a ship; when crises arise, damage can be contained. A "blow-up" in one cell group only affects a relatively small number of people. On the other hand, a problem in a non-cell church can sink the entire local body.

As for me, I pastor a cell church, and I wouldn't have it any other way. People are being discipled and launched into ministry right in their own neighborhoods. They like it, and so do I!

The first step is to clear the initial hurdles. After that, the G-12 system puts your church on a collision course with a destiny I like to call "Mega-Church"!

Rocky J. Malloy

Introduction
Key To Understanding the System

The concept of this book is to take something that appears to be difficult and make it simple.

This book is written for everyone involved in the work of the ministry who desires growth and increase. It is for pastors, missionaries, and ministers of every type. Anyone interested in expanding the Kingdom of Heaven can benefit from the information found within these pages.

This manual isn't exhaustive in the information it provides, but it possesses enough elements for those who wish to embrace the vision. It provides a good "first experience" on the subject of the G-12 cell system within the local church.

More than anything, this book will assist you in realizing your dreams of successful ministry. God doesn't have any mediocre dreams. He dreams big! Yet God also tells you not to despise the day of the small beginnings (Zech. 4:10), because if you are faithful over little, He will trust you with much more (Matt. 25:23).

In order to realize our dreams of success in winning the nations, we must remember two key words: *fruitfulness and multiplication*. These two words are at the core of God's divine plan for man.

God established His will on this matter in Genesis 1:22 when He commanded Adam and Eve to be fruitful and multiply. He is Jehovah Jireh, our Provider, not "Jehovah Fewer," our demise. According to Luke 6:38, He is the God who makes bigger. He adds to what is "pressed down, shaken together and running over"!

"Fruitfulness" speaks of *a gift or a capacity to generate children, one by one* (Ps. 128:3; Gal. 4:19). "Multiplication" also speaks of a gift or a capacity to produce thousands (Gen. 28:3; Deut. 1:10,11). The G-12 cell system provides a very efficient mechanism to increase both our fruitfulness *and* our ability to multiply.

Multiplication is not a choice — it is a divine command! In fact, to make sure there would be no confusion about His desire for us to multiply ourselves, God repeated His command to Noah after the Flood (Gen. 9:1-7). The destruction of the Flood did not change God's will for us. He still intends for us to be fruitful and multiply.

The fruit of a relationship with God is multiplication. For instance, when God spoke to Abraham, He said, "I will multiply your seed" (Gen. 13:16). And in Leviticus 26:9, God once again confirmed His plan to Abraham's descendants, stating, *"I will have respect unto you, and make you fruitful, and multiply you, and establish my covenant with you."*

Let us not allow the devil to confuse us on this matter. To be in a covenant with God means to be fruitful and to multiply.

Somehow the word *small* or poor has come to mean "spiritual" or "holy." The idea that small is better or that quality is more important than quantity is not a biblical principle. If God is involved in something, it is BIG with QUALITY! Quality does not need to be sacrificed in order to be large.

Ministry growth is just like any other promise — you have to see it in the Word in order to believe God for it. I'm here to tell you that ministry growth is definitely in the Word!

If you are still stuck in the mentality that "small is better," look at this scripture:

The Lord your God hath multiplied you, and, behold, ye are this day as the stars of heaven for multitude.
(The Lord God of your fathers make you a thousand times so many more as ye are, and bless you, as he hath promised you!)
Deuteronomy 1:10,11

According to the promises of God, the plan for your church is *big* — a thousand times bigger than it is right now!

We are not talking about money, bread, or fish. We are talking about God's multiplication of men once they are in proper relationship with Him. (If a pastor has thousands of people in his congregation, he will have plenty of money, bread, and fish!)

For too long, church leaders have been satisfied with the status quo instead of reaching out to the lost. Many times, the pastor's desire for big ministry, evangelism, and growth has not been in the heart of the people. In fact, "change" (especially *"big change"*) has almost been a bad word in the Church. The old saying, "We never did it that way before," has sent many a saint to Heaven with less of a reward then what the Father had planned.

Inherent in growth is consistent and constant change! In a growing church, things are constantly changing. In fact, steady, consistent growth is one of the greatest challenges to the local church and to the Church at large.

When revival is sweeping through a region, that is not the time to be a perfectionist. True perfection can only be achieved in death. A corpse is perfectly neat and every hair is in place because it isn't doing anything nor going anywhere. But God isn't looking for churches full of perfectly neat little people. He needs spiritual *hospitals*.

Let me ask you something — do you really think your church can achieve different results when you keep doing the same thing over and over again? A good definition of insanity is to continue doing the same things, yet expecting different results. If you want different results, you must do something *different*.

Acts 6 tells us how God multiplied the Church. Looking back into the first few chapters of Acts, we see that the Church grew first by 3,000 people and then by 5,000 men in one day. This quick growth caused problems. The neat little church of "us four and no more" was completely wiped out when revival hit!

Just think — if you had 5,000 extra people show up this Sunday, would you be prepared?

Pastor Kirkpatrick, who pastors the Florida church where the Brownsville revival broke out, made an interesting observation. He said that when revival started to take place, most of the folks who had been praying for it left the church because of all the newcomers. The church even had to deal with criticism from their denominational headquarters because of all the growth and change.

But revival is not a church service where all the saints sit neatly lined up in the pews. Rather, a revival is where people are overflowing out of the pews into the aisles, sitting on the platform and in chairs lining the walls. The Fire Marshall is trying to shut down the meeting because of fire-code violations, and the police are right behind him to inform the pastor about all the illegally parked cars. It isn't pretty, but it sure is wonderful!

When the G-12 system takes off, you'll have to deal with all kinds of loose ends, but praise God for revival anyway! If you want your church to change for the better, get ready for God to do something big. The end-time harvest is coming, and the G-12 system can get you ready for it.

What does revival mean? Revival is holiness in church life. Revival is keeping the principles of the Word and ministering God's life to others. Revival is walking without carrying the load of sin. It is being full of the joy of the Lord. In Columbia and Brazil, we saw committed people, people with integrity who are serious about the things of God. We saw people full of life! That's what revival is — the genuineness of God's life shining through the Church, drawing in the masses.

In preparation for the masses, you must first understand what a cell is; then you must grab hold of the cell vision for your church. A cell is a fundamental unit of life that finds its origin in God. It is a part of a whole that reproduces thousands and thousands of other cells. The very process of multiplication is what sustains the life of the cell and the body, which the cell helps to form.

We apply the word "cell" to the smallest units of a church *so their purpose of multiplication will never be forgotten.* Cells multiply themselves rapidly and feed themselves in proportion to their multiplication. Every cell has its own functions and special features.

The cell is comprised of God's life, His holiness, and His anointing. It is also comprised of repentance. The cells need these qualities to stay alive. Prayer is the food that keeps the cells healthy, renewed, and committed.

Prayer leads to repentance, which is essential in order for the cells to remain in the fullness of God's life. If the cell is kept healthy, it continues to reproduce itself. But if the leadership rebels or weakens, the cell body becomes cancerous, and its health is threatened. Satan will work to attack the nucleus, or the leadership, of the cell. He knows that he may be able to destroy the whole body if he can get to the head.

That is why we have to stay alert (Eph. 6:18). You see, the G-12 cell system is more than just "family groups," "home churches," or "Bible studies." Each cell is a complete, functioning body, interrelated and supporting the other cells, much like our wonderfully made human bodies, which are made whole in Christ.

This healthy "body" is maintained through holy fellowship. The cell leader is the disciple's friend, his brother in Christ. Discipleship may be explained as "an investment of one's life" or "the ministering of life to others." True discipleship enables the disciple to receive God's life into his life so he can grow spiritually. Then in turn, the disciple begins to multiply, thereby multiplying the cells.

Isaiah 54:2, 3 encompasses this divine call to multiply:

Enlarge the place of thy tent, and let them stretch forth the curtains of thine habitations: spare not, lengthen thy cords, and strengthen thy stakes;
For thou shalt break forth on the right hand and on the left, and thy seed shall inherit the Gentiles, and make the desolate cities to be inhabited.

The goal of this book is to help you discover the simple plan God has for His Church. The G-12 cell system is the example Jesus gave to the Church. It is God's divine plan so the local church might multiply itself. It is a governing system that works.

This book is dedicated to every pastor, missionary, or traveling minister who desires to make room for the multitudes ordained by God to come into the Church in these last days. If you have ever asked God how to help your ministry grow, this book is for you.

The Vision
Chapter 1

God has commissioned us for the purpose of realizing the manifestation of the sons of God (Rom. 8:19). Those of us who walk according to that purpose have vision. Our lives are blessed, and we are fulfilled. The vision is this: To serve God in a greater way by becoming even better servants; to fulfill all He has for us to do, understanding that His desire is not only our personal growth in Him, but also the increase of His family in general.

Only those who have experienced rebirth — who have been born again — are true children of God (John 3:3, 5). You may ask, "But aren't all people children of God?" The Bible clearly answers that question with a resounding NO! To think otherwise is Unitarianism. Only those who receive Jesus Christ as Lord and Savior become children of God (John 1:12). *Therefore, the vision is to save the lost* — those who are wandering aimlessly to hell.

That is why we have local churches — to train every child of God into a leader so he or she can find a God-ordained place in the Body of Christ and save souls from eternal damnation. Jesus commissioned His entire Body to be His disciples. He wants every single member to become effective at accomplishing His will. However, if that is to happen, each disciple must become a discipler (Matt. 28:19). We call that the Great Commission. The G-12 cell system is the way to get there.

To implement the G-12 cell system, we must shatter all that is conventional. Anything that retards growth or keeps us from seeing what is effective must be discarded. If *big* is the will of God (and we know it is), we must look honestly at why we are not as large as we have been called to be. What is keeping us from enlarging our houses as God commands in Isaiah 54:2?

A vision for growth will break through many traditional or conventional church frontiers. To the surprise of many a saint, however, reaching the lost is not the priority of most of today's churches.

What do I mean by "traditional" or "conventional"? Just this:

• Regarding the past as the only sufficient solution for the present and the future.
• Thinking that God can only work in the present the same way He did in the past.
• Limiting God's actions to human hopes, philosophies, and perspectives.

The greatest threat to the widespread acceptance of the G-12 vision is the current vision of the Church, which is not producing sons of God. The current vision — the way we have done it in the past — doesn't have the capacity to accept a different vision.

The apostolic vision that started your church is not necessarily the same vision your church needs to fulfill its call of winning its city and nation for the Lord. However, there is a "pride question" that must be answered: Is the head of the local church willing to say, "There is a better way," as the twelve apostles did in Acts 6:1-7? Would he or she have the courage to say, "What we have been doing is not working"?

In 1998, Pastor Rene de Araújo Terra Nova of International Restoration Ministry in Manaus, Brazil, had the guts to tell his 6,000-member congregation that the vision needed to change. Today he has a congregation of 20,000 people.

Through the G-12 vision, more than 1,000,000 believers have been added to the Brazilian church in only the last few years. That is more growth than the American Church has realized in the past 20 years. *It is time for a change!*

Jesus declared: *"...Why do ye also transgress the commandment of God by your tradition?"* (Matt. 15:3). Traditionalism generates hypocrisy in human beings. It uses the power of argument instead of the power of the Holy Spirit and thereby limits the power of God (Zech. 4:6). Many times traditionalism bears the responsibility for killing the vision, thus destroying the hopes for a victorious future and suffocating our dreams. *"Having a form of godliness, but denying the power thereof..."* (2 Tim. 3:5), traditionalism stagnates and annihilates any hope for better results.

Have you ever seen a church prosper or grow that doesn't go beyond the conventional ways? Certainly not! God wants His people far away from man's tradition. He wants them involved in the movement of the Holy Spirit so they might unleash a great revival (1 Thess. 5:19-21).

We understand that there is only one vision of God and that it is unchangeable: *For God sent not his Son into the world to condemn the world; but THAT THE WORLD THROUGH HIM MIGHT BE SAVED"* (John 3:17). I believe the strategy to fulfill that vision is very plain and is based on the "model of 12" that Jesus gave to His disciples in order to fulfill Matthew 28:19 and 20:

Go ye therefore, and teach all nations, baptizing them in the name of the Father, and of the Son, and of the Holy Ghost: Teaching them to observe all things whatsoever I have commanded you: and, lo, I am with you always, even unto the end of the world. Amen.

The "model of 12" Jesus gave us can be summed up this way: As a group member, you should find a leader you can trust and submit yourself to him, serving as unto the Lord. If you are a leader, find 12 people who trust you as a leader and pour yourself into them, requiring them to do the same for their own group of 12.

G-12 is essentially a cell system based on the "model of 12," meaning 12 people or couples grouped together under a single leader. Each member of the 12 is a leader of his (or her) own group of 12.

Thus, the G-12 uses techniques similar to those Jesus used while He was on earth. What greater pattern could we have than the legacy left by the Master Himself? Jesus trained a group of 12 disciples so they could then reproduce His efforts. The wonderful thing about the implementation of this divine strategy is that it can be changed, adapted, and enhanced according to the Lord's specific plan for a local ministry.

This book will give you the methods used successfully by large, dynamically growing churches. And although nothing apart from the inspired Scriptures is holy, I would caution you not to drift too far from the pattern given in the previous chapter and throughout this book.

You see, we must remain alert to the direction of the Spirit. If the Holy Spirit moves toward the north, it would be crazy to go south. The effort required would be excessively burdensome. And even if we did obtain some results, those results would have been achieved while in rebellion to the Father.

When I first implemented the G-12 vision in my own church, I believed that some parts were not essential and therefore gave priority to others. That was a *big* mistake! Without knowing it,

I created problems that would show up later on down the road, costing our church precious time in revival.

Therefore, take the vision in as a whole. After successfully implementing that vision, you will be in a position to improve it and pass it along to others.

Let me exhort you to break through the barriers of traditionalism (Matt. 9:16,17) and forsake conformity (Eph. 5:14-16). Then take on the G-12 vision with your whole heart and think BIG, for our God is great!

Vision of the G-12 Cell Church

This vision consists of four steps that we call "The Stairway to Success." We believe these steps to be God's strategy for revival in any country.

1. WIN

And he saith unto them, Follow me, and I will make you fishers of men.
Matthew 4:19

For though I preach the gospel, I have nothing to glory of: for necessity is laid upon me; yea, woe is unto me, if I preach not the gospel!
1 Corinthians 9:16

2. CONSOLIDATE

Wherefore receive ye one another, as Christ also received us to the glory of God.
Romans 15:7

3. DISCIPLE

Being confident of this very thing, that he which hath begun a good work in you will perform it until the day of Jesus Christ.
Romans 15:7

4. SEND

For whosoever shall call upon the name of the Lord shall be saved.
How then shall they call on him in whom they have not believed? and how shall they believe in him of whom they have not heard? and how shall they hear without a preacher? And how shall they preach, except they be sent? as it is written, How beautiful are the feet of them that preach the gospel of peace, and bring glad tidings of good things!
Romans 10:13-15

And then he told them, "You are to go into all the world and preach the Good News to everyone, everywhere."
Mark 16:15 TLB

People are won by means of personal evangelism, through the cells and through "Celebration Services." Their lives are *consolidated* through the Encounters and through participation in cell groups. They are *disciplined* through the Leadership School, through participation in the G-12 cells, and through leading their own Multiplication Cells. Finally, people are sent when they begin to lead their own G-12s, form their own Encounter teams and Leadership Schools, and/or implement the G-12 vision in other cities, states, or nations once they are appointed.

The Four Pillars of Church Multiplication

WIN	CONSOLIDATE	DISCIPLE	SEND
Praying for Three (30 days)	Phone Visit in 24 Hours	Leadership School	Leading a Group of 12
Fasting for Three (30 days)	Personal Contact in Seven Days	Member of a Group of 12	Setting up an Encounter Team
Personal Evangelism	Pre-Encounter	Member of a G-144	Forming a Leadership School
Cell Evangelism	Encounter	Member of a G-1728	Leading a G-144
Celebration Services	Post-Encounter	Leader of a Cell	Leading a G-1728
Ministry Networks	Cell Group Member	Re-Encounter	Leaders' Encounter

When these processes are intensively developed, they contribute greatly to a healthy multiplication within the local church. All the levels are interconnected and interdependent, as we will see in greater detail later in this book.

For the vision to succeed, all four *Pillars of Church Multiplication* must be made known throughout the church. The pillars of multiplication that form each step of the stairway support the adjacent pillars. For that reason, each pillar must be addressed with the same intensity and zeal so church members can be developed into effective fishers of men.

Win
Chapter 2

A few years ago, a well-known Charismatic Christian leader came to the city where I live. During four nights of crusade, I witnessed more than 30,000 people go forward to make public confessions for Christ.

It was exciting to see the Body of Christ come together for such a grand event. I was so excited about all those folks filling up the local churches during the crusade. But what a disappointment when not a single person who prayed to receive Jesus returned to visit my church! After talking with the pastors of the largest churches in town, not one of them received a single family either. (I would add that our church was heavily publicized on both television and radio in preparation for the crusade.)

For the Show or for the Souls?

So, what happened to all those thousands who walked the aisles to receive Christ as their Savior? An even tougher question might be "Was the $300,000 spent on producing the crusade good stewardship?" After months of preparing for this massive crusade, with its enormous crowds and huge altar calls, what happened? Where is the fruit?

According to information I have learned and from my personal experience, only one out of every hundred people responding to an altar call in a crusade or some other form of Christian mass media will ever attend church. Why is it such a low number? Because the people who respond in a mass-media event such as a crusade don't know anyone in the church!

I used to be a marketing director for a large church that spent millions of dollars in advertising. The television budget alone was monstrous. With all that exposure plus giant Christian events and a multimillion-dollar sanctuary, the church was unable to hold on to the people. No matter how many people came through the front door, almost that many left through the back door.

While working at this church, I conducted a little survey on our first-time visitors.

• 10 percent said they attended the church for the first time because of what they had seen on television.
• 5 percent named other avenues of advertisement, such as our radio broadcast, billboards, or direct mail, as the reason they had visited our church.
• An overwhelming 85 percent of the first-time visitors said it was because someone had invited them.

Would you invest your money in the 5-percent return, the 10-percent return, or the 85-percent return? Surprisingly, the American Church keeps pouring billions of dollars into the 5-percent and 10-percent return.

Incredible as it seems, traditional churches put their money into the methods that get the smallest return. Are these churches pursuing souls or prestige? Is their goal to make the pastor's name a household word or to get the Name of Jesus into people's hearts and homes? What is the motivation? Is it a television program, or is it church growth? Is it fame or winning the lost? Answering these questions confirmed to me that cell evangelism is the only way to go.

According to a recent report by the Baptists, it costs about $1,500 per salvation in America for any denomination. Why? Because the invitations people receive to come to church are through the television, radio, or the newspaper, instead of from a friend. Why spend $1,500 per salvation, when the same invitation can be delivered gratis — without charge — through the cell members?

People and relationships are where the emphasis should be. This is why the cell church is superior in retaining souls and multiplying people. The cell church puts the most emphasis on the 85-percent return, which is literally hundreds of times more cost-effective at soul-winning.

"Stranger evangelism" is too costly and ineffective to justify its continued utilization by the church. It is simply bad stewardship. That is why the cell revolution is taking over. It's not only a better, more effective, and less costly way to win souls, but, again, it is also the way Jesus evangelized. The greatest miracle of all is when a lifeless spiritual being becomes a new creature in Christ Jesus through faith (2 Cor. 5:17).

The Words of Your Mouth

According to the Restaurant Association of America, one person has the ability to affect a very large number of people. They say that one bad meal can affect as many as 2,500 patrons! Why? The patron who received the bad meal will tell someone who in turn will tell someone else — until the story has reached out into the community. Word-of-mouth has always been the best or, in some cases, the worst advertisement. Indeed, it has been known to either make or break a new business. If word-of-mouth can work that way in the negative, think of what it can do for the good!

Let's look at the Charmin bathroom tissue commercial. It was one of the most successful ad campaigns in history. People all over the country were talking about squeezing the Charmin. "Squeeze the Charmin" became a cute way to say you were going to the bathroom. The question "Johnny, where are you going?" would produce the response "To squeeze the Charmin,

Mom." It became a household phrase. Long after the ads stopped running, people were still "squeezing the Charmin."

Ask any marketing executive or advertising agent about word-of-mouth advertising. It is the single most powerful tool in marketing. If a product can become a household name, it will become enormously successful.

This same principle works with evangelism. When people start to speak spontaneously about Jesus to their friends and invite them to their cell group or church, it is equal to thousands of dollars of advertising. The end result is more souls saved per dollar spent. Instead of one out of every hundred returning to church after an altar call, it will increase to a phenomenal one out of two!

What would a 50-percent increase in retention do for your church? It is easy to see that if the congregation is not trained and organized, the church limps along on the one percent. But why settle for the traditional one percent instead of the cell-based results of 50 percent?

What message is coming out of the mouths of your congregation? You see, the size of the church or its advertising budget is not really the issue; it's the openness and friendliness of the members that counts. Unfortunately, the friendliest church in the world cannot achieve its goals if the handshake at the front door is not followed up by an invitation to someone's home after the service. Church must move beyond the sanctuary if it wants to grow.

Evangelization through cells is many times more successful than mass media. If the church is behind the cell leadership and will finance their evangelism efforts, I guarantee that the church will grow and multiply.

Evangelization Through Personal Contacts

Personal contacts are powerful. People you already have contact with on a regular basis are the starting point for evangelism. Relationships through family and work are always the easiest to reach because they are people you know. Every time someone comes to Jesus, an entire little community is affected by that salvation. If one bad meal can affect 2,500 people, imagine what the testimony of one sinner coming to Jesus has the potential of accomplishing!

Imagine this: A man through a friend is invited to a cell group meeting. While at this meeting, he receives Jesus as his Lord and Savior. Within a few weeks, that man's life starts to take on some major changes. He feels a need to be more sensitive to the needs of his wife and children. Selfish habits start to fade away in favor of acts on behalf of others. Vices or carnal desires start to give way to a greater need to attend church and get to know God better. He begins to gain control over undesirable qualities in his life.

As a result of all this, those close to the man want to know what is going on in his life. Indeed, they begin to wonder if they might also be changed for the better as he was. Every time a person receives Jesus through this man's testimony, the process starts all over again. I hope you can begin to see how infinitely more powerful this is than any form of mass media.

We are living epistles, or living testimonies, of Christ (2 Cor. 3:2). People start asking us what we have because they see something in us they need and want. You see, evangelizing does not mean knocking someone in the head with the Bible! On the contrary, it is sharing with a person who asks us how they can be changed. It's natural, easy, and fun!

Once a person becomes experienced at testifying to those around him, he will usually become confident enough to begin witnessing to others outside his personal contacts. That is when a cell leader has a soul-winner on his hands!

Read what happened in John 4:39,40 with the Samaritan woman. This lady was such an outcast that the other women wouldn't even collect water with her. She had to go in the heat of the day. Yet after an encounter with the love of Jesus, this woman went to those who despised her of her own initiative and revealed to them the treasure she had found. Although she was an outcast, her convictions won her community over to Jesus. The Bible says, *"And many of the Samaritans of that city believed on him for the saying of the woman, which testified, He told me all that ever I did"* (John 4:39).

It is true that this witnessing process goes on in regular, non-cell churches; however, gaining entry into those churches is tougher. Why is that? Because the traditional church has a hard outer shell, which makes penetration into it more difficult.

No, it is not actually more difficult to walk into a traditional church building. It is, however, more difficult to find your place in the existing "society" of the church. Weaving through the maze of special-interest groups and little cliques can be quite a chore. That's why so few people are actually added to the Body of Christ after all the crusades, special events, and advertising.

On the other hand, a cell church has an easy entry threshold. The soft spot is the home meetings. A home environment is much less intimidating than a church. Remember, the number-one reason new people drop out of church is that they haven't made any friends.

I cannot stress enough the importance of relationships. They are imperative, not only for new growth, but also for increased church attendance and participation. Without relationships, the newcomer grows cold and eventually drops out, leaving the church on a negative note. Thus, instead of the new convert reaching his community for Christ, he becomes a dropout statistic. That happens to 99 out of every 100 people. Most churches' solution to this problem is to spend more money instead of instituting a superior strategy.

Don't make that same mistake. Make your harvesting efficient by building relationships through Multiplication Cells. These positive relationships in turn will spawn more positive relationships as the cell church grows.

Evangelization Through Cell Vision Or Like Interest

Every Multiplication Cell has a vision for direction, motivation, and evangelization. The Multiplication Cell is such a tremendous tool for evangelism because it has the potential for attracting people outside Christian circles — people whose family and friends have no religious heritage. Cell vision has the ability to draw in those who are unchurched and who would never be reached any other way.

In the church I pastor, I try to help leaders choose positive objectives that are based on victorious visions versus negative ones. For example, instead of having a "divorcees' group," we call it a "singles' group." Instead of having a "cancer patients' group," we have both an "intercessors' group" and another called the "hospital visitation group." Practically speaking, it is more effective for a person believing for healing to join a group that visits hospitals or intercedes for the sick than it is for him to join a group believing for his healing. As Acts 20:35 says,

"...It is more blessed to give than to receive." Also, what happens when these people dealing with cancer get healed? Do they leave their friends in the hospital visitation or the intercessors' group? No!

That is why instead of a "single moms' group," you could have a "parents' group." That way, when one of the mothers gets married, she can still stay in the same group.

Therefore, always keep the group's vision positive if at all possible. I know there may be exceptions to this principle, but consider how powerful it is to belong to a positive group instead of a "need" group, which by definition is making the statement that God has not supplied *"...according to his riches in glory..."* (Phil. 4:19). It is always better to stay in faith than in need.

A cell vision disarms people. It helps lower their defenses, making it easier to receive Christ. A cell vision establishes a common interest upon which to establish communication until the greater reason, Jesus, can emerge.

From the standpoint of evangelism, however, it is also important that the focus of the cell never compromise righteousness or integrity. To make an exaggerated point, a group's vision would never be to establish an international beer club or a satanic rock group just because it would reach unchurched people!

Did you know that three years after salvation, the average saint only knows three unsaved people? Can you see why churches grow old and stale? After only a few years, the new Christian has cocooned himself in a comfortable society called Christianity. He listens to Christian music, attends Christian events, and shops in Christian friends' stores.

But reaching outside that community is an absolute necessity if the Church is to grow. Cell vision facilitates our continued contact with the outside world.

In my younger days, just the Name of Jesus was enough to totally intimidate me. I believe that's why there are so many names for God, like the "man upstairs." There are all kinds of inappropriate labels people use that don't at all define or describe God. But people without a personal relationship with God find it intimidating to speak about the Father, the Son, or the Holy Ghost.

That's why it is helpful to have something else to talk about besides God in a Multiplication Cell meeting. This allows friendships to develop because it lowers the confrontation level, making it easier for both parties to communicate when the right time comes. All "like interest" really does is provide a platform for friendship. Talking to a stranger about a common interest can cause an interest in one another to grow, which in turn often develops into friendship. It all boils down to the importance of fellowship and personal relationships.

Reaching outsiders through like interests is a little more challenging than reaching family and friends. It requires more training and a greater resolve.

I enjoy finding like interests with people everywhere I go. If I'm in a cab, I talk to the driver about cars. If I'm in a restaurant, I talk to the waiter about service or food. If I meet someone in the grocery store, I open up with comments about what they are buying. Over the years, I have literally led thousands of people to the Lord in the streets, in grocery stores, in cabs, in restaurants and, of course, in church by finding a common denominator to begin a conversation. I find it fun and challenging. You will too.

Winning Strategy for Meetings

In any meeting where there is a newcomer, it is always advised to close the meeting with a prayer of salvation unless the Holy Spirit leads in a different way. Always give a sinner the chance to confess Jesus as his or her Lord and Savior (Rom. 10:9). Never miss an opportunity to lead someone to salvation.

I'm sure every minister has his way of doing this, but I have personally found that the most effective way is to ask the entire congregation to stand up and confess, word for word, a prayer of repentance and salvation. This reinforces the commitment of those praying for the first time, and it gives the others a chance to practice saying the prayer so they can repeat it with someone else when the opportunity arises.

After everyone has prayed, ask those in the congregation who prayed this prayer for the first time to raise their hands in order to receive a specific prayer for them. Then ask them to leave their chairs and come forward

Every step of this process involves a phase along the road to these people's resurrection. The first step is a collective prayer. The second step is a decision to expose themselves, coming to the front in order to receive a specific prayer. After a brief exhortation, bring the new converts to the realization of their need to assume a new life in Christ.

Some think this technique is too intimidating, especially when the target is unchurched people. I have found it very profitable to help people make that big decision for salvation by gently urging them to receive.

The nonbelievers who come to the cell meetings or Celebration Services arrive dead in their trespasses and sins. Many times they are not in a condition to make a decision without help (Eph. 2:1). Therefore, the Holy Spirit will work with you, gently guiding those who don't know the Lord to make the right decision.

At this moment, these people should be asked to turn around and look at the congregation. (Before, they were facing the preacher with their backs to the audience.) The preacher then presents the new believers to the church — their new family in Christ.

The entire church then celebrates, clapping hands in praise to God for those new believers. They sing songs of joy, show banners, and welcome their new brothers and sisters with great enthusiasm. The dynamics are fabulous! Many cry when they see how warmly the church welcomes them (Rom. 15:7).

The consolidation leader must be available to guide the new converts to a separate room, where the consolidation process begins. As they leave the sanctuary, the congregation keeps on celebrating.

Once in a separate room, the members of the consolidation team share with the new believers concerning the sincerity of their decision to follow Jesus. They do so by informing them that they are now God's children and that Jesus lives in their hearts. They also receive an explanation about what it means to be a new creature in Christ Jesus (2 Cor. 5:17).

After that, the new converts are quizzed about whether they are children of God and where Jesus lives. It is important that they respond correctly. If they don't, those ministering to them should continue until the new converts understand what just happened in their lives. It is crucial that they confess Jesus as Lord and Savior and *not just repeat a prayer that means nothing to them.*

After this, cards are filled out to obtain enough information about the new converts that the consolidation team can properly follow up. Once the consolidation group has confirmed that the new converts are sincere, a specific prayer is said over the entire group of new believers. The following declaration is then made:

From now on, you are no longer simple creatures. You are now God's children, for the Bible declares in John 1:12, "But as many as received him, to them gave he power to become the sons of God, even to them that believe on his name."

As children of God, you possess rights in the house of your Father. I want to explain these rights to you:

1. You have the right to pray and know that your prayers will be heard.

2. You have the right to hear God's voice through reading the Bible, which is His Word (John 14:13; 1 Peter 2:1, 2). If you don't own a Bible, purchase one immediately, because all the promises the Bible contains are there for you. Eventually you will also be able to properly discern God's voice, as He talks to you personally and prophetically.

3. You are not alone anymore. You have a family of many new friends, brothers, and sisters who are waiting to meet you.

The group is then led back to the sanctuary. There the congregation is waiting and excited to greet them and to warmly welcome them into the Body of Christ. (Don't ask those wanting to confirm their salvation to go forward to the front of the church when the aisles are jammed with people trying to leave. Also, please instruct the congregation that salvation is more important than being the first one out of the parking lot.)

Through these procedures, many people can be set free from the bondage of sin to see the light of Christ's Gospel. With each new beginning, the consolidation process has started once again.

Intercessory Prayer for the Lost

In intercessory prayer, you present yourself before God on behalf of the people (Ezek. 22:30; Dan. 9:3). It is ideal to intercede for individuals who wish to be taken to church. There they will have the opportunity to say the prayer of deliverance. They will be consolidated and subsequently cared for and edified.

Now let's apply what we learn from the following teachings.

There were present at that season some that told him of the Galilaeans, whose blood Pilate had mingled with their sacrifices.
And Jesus answering said unto them, Suppose ye that these Galilaeans were sinners above all the Galilaeans, because they suffered such things?
I tell you, Nay: but, except ye repent, ye shall all likewise perish.
Or those eighteen, upon whom the tower in Siloam fell, and slew them, think ye that they were sinners above all men that dwelt in Jerusalem?
I tell you, Nay: but, except ye repent, ye shall all likewise perish.
Luke 13:1-5

In Luke 12, Jesus had been teaching on judgment. Those He was teaching piped up when they heard this. "Yes," they said, "that happened to some Galileans. Pilate killed them while they were worshiping!"

However, the judgment Jesus was talking about was not a righteous judgment but rather the accusations of Satan. Jesus straightened out the people's religious beliefs and helped those listening to understand that the reason bad things happen to good people is not necessarily because of sin.

Jesus sought to establish that point by giving another example of 18 people who died in an accident. He asked, "Do you think the Galileans or the 18 victims were worse sinners than anyone else?" Then He told the people listening that this kind of thinking was dangerous and that they needed to repent before something worse happened to them.

Jesus continued His teaching by using a parable, which is a natural example of a spiritual principle:

He spoke also this parable; A certain man had a fig tree planted in his vineyard; and he came and sought fruit thereon, and found none.
Then said he unto the dresser of his vineyard, Behold, these three years I come seeking fruit on this fig tree, and find none: cut it down; why cumbereth it the ground?
And he answering said unto him, Lord, let it alone this year also, till I shall dig about it, and dung it:
And if it bear fruit, well: and if not, then after that thou shalt cut it down.
Luke 13:6-9

Jesus used this parable to teach that the difference between bad things happening or not happening is not necessarily dependent on whether or not there is sin in someone's life; it can also be the result of intercession or the lack thereof. You see, we are all guilty, and we all deserve to die (Rom. 3:23). Through our sin, we have all earned the death penalty.

So why does the pastor's wife die and the town bully survive three car wrecks and half a dozen drug overdoses? According to Jesus' teaching, the difference was intercession! The town bully's grandmother kept her grandson constantly bathed in prayer. As for the pastor's wife, she was not sufficiently covered by prayer for the position she held in the Body of Christ. One tree had the reinforcing strength of fertilizer — a fervent intercessor. The other did not.

Volumes could be written about these nine verses, but that is beyond the scope of this book. My point here is to demonstrate that intercession is an extremely powerful tool; it can mean the difference between life and death. However, all the intercession in the world, if not backed up with a presentation of the Gospel, will save no one. Rom. 10:14 says, *"...How shall they hear without a preacher?"*

Intercession builds a spiritual fortress around a person. Once the person is under the protection of the Lord, one of three things will happen:

• One, the peace that results from being in that safe place in the Lord will draw that person to the Gospel. Rom. 2:4 says, *"...the goodness of God leadeth thee to repentance."*

• Two, the walls of the fortress will deny the sinner the pleasures of sin, which are only for a season. This will drive a wedge of separation between him and his sin. The loss of the pleasures of this world will drive the rebellious sinner to repentance.

• Third, the tenacious will of the sinner to go to hell will override all efforts on his behalf, no matter how long he lives.

The odds are that this person will succumb to the power in intercession and give his heart to God.

When interceding, it is imperative that you stand on the promises of God. The following are some verses for different situations concerning repentance and acceptance.

And they said, Believe on the Lord Jesus Christ, and THOU SHALT BE SAVED, AND THY HOUSE.
Acts 16:31

The Lord is not slack concerning his promise, as some men count slackness; but is long-suffering to us-ward, not WILLING THAT ANY SHOULD PERISH, BUT THAT ALL SHOULD COME TO REPENTANCE.
2 Peter 3:9

For the Son of man is come to save that which was lost.
Matthew 18:11

Therefore, behold, I will hedge up thy way with thorns, and make a wall, that she shall not find her paths.
And she shall follow after her lovers, but she shall not overtake them; and she shall seek them, but shall not find them: then shall she say, I WILL GO AND RETURN TO MY FIRST HUSBAND; FOR THEN WAS IT BETTER WITH ME THAN NOW.
Hosea 2:6, 7

The Prayer for Three

The most powerful weapon we have from the Lord is prayer. We must use it with intelligence to obtain the expected results (1 John 5:1-15; Col. 4:2, 3).

"Prayer for three" involves focused intercession for 30 days by one dedicated person, each praying and fasting for the same three persons during that entire time. It has proven extremely effective because it is taken right from the Word of God in

Matthew 18:16-20. As I mentioned earlier, intercession binds spiritual strongholds and releases the Spirit of God to work powerfully on behalf of those to whom the prayer is directed. It also sets short-term goals with achievable victory.

After the 30 days of intercession, the person who has prayed in agreement shares the Gospel with the three for whom he or she has been praying. The results are impressive! Why? Because *"...the EFFECTUAL FERVENT PRAYER of a righteous man availeth much"* (James 5:16). Intercession also allows one to put his faith to work: *"...Faith, if it hath not works, is dead, being alone"* (James 2:17).

Daniel 9 and 10 provides a biblical example of how powerful intercessory prayer can be. Daniel changed the direction of a nation with the following four steps of intercession:

1. Take a sincere personal interest in the people you are praying for (Dan. 9:3).

2. Confess the people's sins as if they were your own (Dan. 9:5).

3. Implore God's mercy (Dan. 9:18).
4. Persevere in prayer. Don't back off until the answer comes (Dan. 10:10-14).

Knowing these basic principles, we can perform the following prayer mechanics:

1. Daily commitment of intercessory prayer (1 Thess. 5:17; Eph. 6:18).

2. Weekly team intercession.

3. Prayer pact between three other people (Gal. 6:2). This is when the first three cell members and the leader each pray for three additional members in order to complete their cell group of 12.

The Goal of Evangelization Is Discipleship

Peter said evangelization without proper follow-up could leave a person worse than when we found them (2 Peter 2:20-22). For a long time, I didn't understand how someone could get saved and then be worse off. But after several years of being a pastor, I can now tell you how it happens. If we allow a new convert to go back into the world, they can become hardened to the Gospel, making it very difficult to draw them into discipleship the second or third time around.

The lost are the devil's property (John 8:44). The devil loses a soul the moment he comes to Christ. Satan gets revenge on the new believer by targeting that person with attacks (Matt. 12:45). If he is successful, not only can the salvation of that soul be placed in jeopardy, but that person can become a bad testimony in the community and keep others from salvation.

That is why the baby Christian *must* be discipled. He cannot be left alone to face the devil without any training or preparation. That is also why the Bible says we are to study to show ourselves approved (2 Tim. 2:15). Approved for what? Approved for victory over the wiles of the enemy (Eph. 6:11).

One reason the Bible calls us sheep is that we need to stay together in flocks. Once we are cut off from the pastor and from fellowship with the saints, we are easy targets for wolves.

Suppose that after a giant crusade, a newly born-again couple finds their way to church. Statistically, they will drop out in less than a month if they don't make any Christian friends. Enormous crusades and the mass media all sow the Word, but experiencing conversion with a trusted friend will perform the miraculous.

In no way does this suggest that a prayer for salvation is any less real if it is prayed in a crusade or as a result of ministry through some form of mass media. I am simply saying that when a person passes from spiritual death to spiritual life, it is important for that person to have someone walk through it with him.

I stress again: Church is all about relationships. The more relationships a person develops and cultivates in church, the greater the likelihood is that they will stay long enough to see fruit produced in their lives. The cell church fosters and develops relationships so people can feel comfortable about being discipled.

The Great Commission, as set forth by Christ, was to make disciples of all nations. In order for us to reach this goal, we *must* evangelize. Evangelism is not an end, but a means to that end. It is a step in the process of fulfilling Jesus' last command.

The most effective evangelism and discipleship is always one on one. Cell evangelism is so effective for this very reason. Instead of "cold-calling" strangers at the end of a crusade, you make new friends in someone's living room. The Multiplication Cell structure greatly facilitates entry-level discipleship because it provides minimum confrontation evangelism opportunities with built-in follow-up procedures. (It is a lot easier to call on someone who is waiting for your call than it is to call a stranger who is trying to avoid you.)

In Summary

Winning souls is the pure and simple preaching of the Gospel, which must be done by every disciple of Jesus Christ (Rom. 10:14,15). Volumes have been written on this subject. However, books on soul-winning are like books on exercising: A lot of people have them but few put them to work!

The Church should not lose the opportunity to win the largest number of people possible for God's Kingdom (Matt. 4:19). To do this, believers will have to stay constantly motivated.

Once a group of 12 had been completed, the members will want to complete their G-144, G-1,728 and G-20,736 more than ever. At that point, it will be necessary to go beyond the four walls of the church and reach out to the lost. As they do so, they will grow, their cells will grow, and the church at large will grow!

The supreme objective of this vision is to win souls. It is God's burning desire that His children are saved. We need to take advantage of all the opportunities (2 Tim. 4:2) — at the Network Meetings, at the main Celebration Services, by personal evangelism, and in the Multiplication Cells that meet in offices, factories, schools, and homes.

Don't you want everyone to go to Heaven? Don't you want everyone to enjoy the peace that passes all understanding, here and now in this life?

The bottom line is this: If we really love what God loves, we love people. So then the question arises, "How can we receive the masses into the family of God?" Or, more importantly, we should ask, "How can we bring people into a relationship with God if we are not willing to enter into a relationship with them?"

Consolidate
Chapter 3

The vision of *"Win, Consolidate, Disciple, and Send"* has been revolutionary — a revival with a method!

The Church has been winning souls ever since the resurrection of Jesus Christ, but it has been weak in its consolidation and discipleship, especially for the last 1,500 years. Then the Lord gave Pastor Cesar Castellano a vision of why Jesus was so successful. Since then, the revelation of "consolidating and discipling" has turbo-charged the efforts of the Church.

In a very short time, the principles of the G-12 have *added* — *not swapped* or stolen — hundreds of thousands of unsaved people to the Church. In Brazil alone, using this G-12 system, more than a million souls have been added to the Church in just the last two years. That is more real growth than the American Church has seen in decades!

Missions Charismatic International Church is enormously successful. People are flying in every day to see what the people of this church are doing and how they are doing it. They are extremely well-organized with loyal and dedicated leaders. The church has more than 100,000 members and is still growing. The key to it all is the consolidation process.

The Heart of the Vision

The heart of the G-12 vision can be found in Romans 15:7: *"Wherefore receive ye one another, as Christ also received us to the glory of God."* Every single person, man, woman, and child is considered a leader in the G-12 vision. Children ten years of age have their own G-12s. Everyone is treated like a winner, and it shows.

Consolidation starts when a person says "yes" to Jesus and ends when the person is dropped off at the door of discipleship. During the process, the new believer is planted firmly in the house of God. The entire procedure happens so efficiently that the new believer has little chance of being offended or backsliding. Before he realizes it, he's leading first a G-12, then a G-144, and, finally, a G-1728. In other words, consolidation closes the holes in the net.

Not losing 99 percent of the visitors is actually a huge shock to the system. That is why the G-12 is so challenging. The dramatic growth resulting from not losing is enough to jump-start a church into revival.

Think of it in terms of money. If a business has been losing millions of dollars every day, just stopping the loss would be equal to millions of dollars in extra revenue. It would pole-vault a company forward without its actually earning a dime more of profit!

That's why consolidation is such a tremendous strategy. It closes the back door of the church, which dramatically affects church growth. Thus, the entire G-12 vision revolves around the core of consolidation.

Exposure Time

Speed and efficiency are the keys. In the G-12 vision, a six-month-old Christian is producing fruit, not drinking milk because he is in the Word. The dynamics are tremendous! A new convert is taken from conversion to Leadership School in less than six months. Instead of the church being a giant baby-sitting service, it becomes a fortress for sending troops into battle.

Have you noticed the strategy many of the mega-churches have adopted in order to keep their people? They have water parks, bowling alleys, sports gyms, play lands — all kinds of extravaganzas. Imagine — people are being martyred for the sake of the Gospel in various places on this earth as you read this book. Yet we have to offer million-dollar amusements just to keep our folks in church!

Instead of investing billions of dollars to simply maintain the "nursery," the G-12 system puts soldiers in the field who bring the spoils into the house of God within six months! In some circles, a six-month-old Christian would be considered a baby. In the G-12 system, they are lieutenants in the Army of God.

It is easy to see why it takes $1,500 per salvation in America. With the G-12 system, instead of spending church funds on giant milk bottles, the money goes toward evangelization, consolidation, discipleship, and sending out emissaries to ignite the process all over again in other locations. It all happens so quickly that the new Christian learns how to love and respect authority instead of how to criticize the pastor. He learns discipline instead of laziness. He learns how to edify instead of how to destroy, and he learns how to produce instead of how to suck the bottle.

In the non-G-12 churches, the process of bringing a saint to maturity takes so long that the losses are outrageous. It has to do with the time of exposure — the longer the exposure time, the greater the risk.

For example, did you know that skydiving is less dangerous than scuba diving? Scuba diving doesn't look more dangerous, but the difference is the time of exposure. Skydiving has less than two minutes of exposure to risk; scuba diving has 30 minutes or more. In the G-12 system, the new Christian's "time of exposure" to offense is cut way back, which automatically results in a lesser risk of losing him to the world. Thus, cutting back the time of exposure on the track of maturity serves to catapult growth because it dramatically cuts losses.

Getting Started

A person who responds to the invitation to accept Jesus as his Savior should be walked through the prayer of salvation, a confession of his faith, the presentation of his rights as a child of God, and a reinforcement of his confession, if needed. Afterward, a salvation card for the new believer should be filled out. Even though salvation can occur in different settings such as Celebration Services, Multiplication Cells, or outreaches, the consolidation process is the same. In every case, the information on the salvation card is needed to start the process.

However, this salvation card doesn't have to be something requiring huge bureaucratic maneuvers. A simple card requesting sufficient information so the person can be contacted (preferably at home) will do fine. This information card should then be passed out liberally to the congregation, especially to the Multiplication Cell leaders who are still consolidating their groups.

1. It is critical to explain to the new believer why the salvation card must be filled out accurately before he begins to write down information. The salvation card is so very important. Without it, there can be no consolidation, no "next step" in his new life in Jesus. Therefore, the information written on the card about the new believer must be sufficient to allow the initiation of consolidation to begin.

If the information on the card is not correct, you might lose contact with a "babe in Christ." If the person does not understand the reason he is filling out the card, he may give the wrong information, thinking that he might be approached later for money or sought after for carnal reasons.

That is why we highly recommend that all evangelism and the initial steps of consolidation be done by a person who is the same gender as the new believer. It is not appropriate for a man to ask for a woman's home address, phone number, or other personal information.

2. Contact the new believer by phone within 24 hours. If you pray for someone to accept Christ in the grocery store, at least get his or her phone number and call the person the next day. The phone call is vital because it is the first step toward developing a relationship with the person who has just entered into his or her new life. If at all possible, during that phone conversation, make an appointment to visit the person's home that same week.

PRE-ENCOUNTER— DISCOVERY?

3. During that first visit, offer the new believer free literature that adequately explains what has happened to him, and invite him to participate in the Pre-Encounter. The Pre-Encounter will explain what salvation is and what is necessary for him to do if he wants to remain on track with God.

4. The Encounter and Post-Encounter follow the Pre-Encounter.

5. Once the new believer has participated in the Pre-Encounter and the Encounter, the next step is participation in a Multiplication Cell — if he is not already attending one.

The goal of consolidation is to establish the image of Christ in the believer and to expose him to the leader within himself. Consolidation produces solid, stable, confirmed, and reaffirmed Christians.

Remember, consolidation is a call of God to comfort the weak (1 Thess. 5:14). It is a ministry of consolation, comfort, and reconciliation. We shouldn't forget that we are reaching out to a hurting and dying world. Not all the fish will jump into the boat; it takes a little work. The more we do it, the better we will become at hauling in the net.

We shouldn't get discouraged if at first we meet with disappointment. We cannot force anyone to be saved; neither can we consolidate anyone into the Body of Christ. All we can ever do is show the way and ask people to follow. Sometimes we can push a little, but never manipulate! Our lives are to be an open book, transparent and visible, so that the new convert can look right through us (2 Cor. 3:2, 3). The greater intimacy we have with God, the greater our ability to attract people to the Lord.

Completing the entire consolidation process is powerful, because it blesses the consolidator as much as the one being consolidated. Witnessing the life of God being established in someone is truly exciting. It makes one desire to help more people to do the same thing.

Years ago, in the streets of Havana, I had prayed for about 2,000 people to accept Christ. While flying back from Cuba, the word of the Lord came to me. He told me that the laws of nature are not *canceled* by spiritual law, but rather *superseded* by them. The Lord went on to say that every time we pray for someone's salvation, the eternal life of God that enters that person passes through us.

One of the laws of nature is this: *For every action, there is an opposite and equal reaction.* Every time you pray for the salvation of a person or bring him or her through a consolidation process, the very thing that happens to that person is also happening to you. So if you want to stay young, win souls!

No one should receive God's life and keep it for himself. Believers are to multiply their blessings by pouring themselves into the lives of others.

Consolidation involves the whole church. Answering the call to consolidate brings holiness into the entire congregation (Heb. 12:14). Consolidation teaches the local body of believers to love the lost, to set the captives free with the Word of Life, and to develop a true faith and a genuine interest in the well-being of others.

Wise Follow-up

Consolidation is really just another word for intense follow-up. The goal of all follow-up is the same — to produce a disciple of Christ. Evangelism brings the lost into contact with Christ; follow-up focuses on *making* a disciple. Finally, discipleship involves training a person to be successful at both evangelism and follow-up.

People who are being consolidated can be placed in one of three categories:

- The unchurched, (which usually means the lost)
- People looking for another church
- Those involved in cults, Satanism, or false religion

The challenge of follow-up or consolidation is to let the new convert know he is special to God without pestering or annoying him. If the new believer is suffering from self-condemnation, guilt, or fear, even a kind letter of invitation or a friendly call might be perceived as pushy.

The real key to follow-up is to know just how hard to push and to know just when to stop. That is why a salvation in a cell group has a definite advantage over a church service. When a person gives his life to Christ in the intimacy of a backyard or living room, the group's leader has greater insight into the character and personality of the person being ministered to than when the same thing happens in a Celebration Service. For that reason, the preferred location for salvation is in the Multiplication Cell.

Consolidating new believers who are friends and family members is a little different than consolidating people outside that circle. When people's friends or acquaintances are drawn into the church, follow-up is natural. They are already in regular communication with their loved ones, motivating and encouraging them.

However, follow-up with a new acquaintance involves more dedication and energy. The best motivation is a common interest. That is why cell vision is so vital. The "Jesus connection" is often too intense for people, especially for the unchurched. A conversation about computers or children, followed by a gentle reminder about the next week's meeting, is much more comfortable for most people.

When a person commits to attend a meeting (especially a cell meeting), but doesn't show up, this situation must be handled delicately. It almost always requires a personal visit. One definite "no-no" is to ask the person where he was at the time of the meeting. That is a very confrontational question. The person knows why you are paying him a visit. You don't need to compound the guilt or condemnation by asking difficult questions.

So what do you do in a situation like that? Initiate a light conversation — one in which you casually bring up how the meeting went and what it did for you personally. This will go much further than condemnation.

Anyone who is not in Christ is hurting and needs help. Many are so lost that they don't know where to start. A personal visit will go a long way in establishing trust and friendship with a person who is outside Christendom.

Fears and anxieties keep people from fulfilling their commitments, but a Christian friend can be an entrance into a new world of hope for a new believer. Therefore, reinforcing hope and love will do more than anything else to establish someone in Christ. Condemnation is the very reason many never go to church in the first place.

There are many reasons people look around for another church. In my experience, "program-based" churchgoers usually experiment with a cell church because they are looking for fellowship and greater fulfillment in their Christian walk. This group is both the most unique and the most difficult, and, for various reasons, is definitely not the target group. The people in this category often arrive with all kinds of emotional baggage and require a great deal of counseling and love.

People usually don't leave a church if they are fulfilled and content. Therefore, when you take in people from other churches, that usually means taking in those who are hurting and offended. The very institution they went to for help has hurt them. Unlike new believers who are fresh and excited, those who "come from another church" are often feeling disheartened when they start attending your church. It is therefore best to have the more mature believers work with this group.

However, this group is actually the easiest to follow up on because they already know what it is to make a commitment to a local body. The real work with this group starts with discipleship. A strong orientation about how cells work and the vision of the church is critical to the successful consolidation of people coming in from other churches.

Lastly, people coming out of a cult form the third group. People involved in cults are often sincere about serving God; however, they have been deceived. The fact that they have attended a cell meeting, Celebration Service, or any Christian meeting or service outside their own "church" means a significant breakthrough has occurred in their lives. It also means they are going through a very fearful time.

It can be very difficult, and sometimes even dangerous, for a person who is trying to escape a cult such as the Jehovah's Witnesses, Mormons, Bahaís, Satanism, or witchcraft (just to name a few). Those who remain in the cult often instigate intense persecution against the person desiring to leave. Knowing what to do to shelter victims of cults requires much more information than this book can contain. Suffice it to say that anyone coming out of a cult needs special attention and aggressive follow-up.

Once the consolidation process has begun, it is very important that the process is followed through to its completion. Completion of the consolidation process occurs when the convert is in discipleship and attending a cell group and church faithfully. Until these things occur, follow-up continues.

If follow-up on a new believer has continued for more than two months without any success, this usually means the person is trying to relay the message, "Don't bother me anymore." However, follow-up on those who have come out of cults may need to go on for much longer than for those who come from other churches. The goal is not to rustle sheep, but to save the lost.

The Three Phases of Consolidation

There are three phases to the consolidation process: the *Pre-Encounter*, the *Encounter*, and the *Post-Encounter*. Each phase has a very special purpose, and all are necessary if consolidation is to be complete. In these Encounters, which are directed by trained leadership, participants see the power of God mightily at work building the church!

PRE-ENCOUNTER

The new convert will be consolidated by his discipler and directed toward the Pre-Encounter. Men, women, and young adults may attend the Pre-Encounter together; children and adolescents have their own Encounters. The Pre-Encounter is subdivided into four meetings, each taking place once a week and lasting exactly one hour. For some churches, it works better to complete the Pre-Encounter in two two-hour sessions over a period of two weeks.

The subjects of the four sessions are as follows:

• Sin and Its Results
• The First Adam and the Last Adam — Death and Resurrection
• We Are Saints and Sons of God
• Who We Are in Christ Jesus

These meetings are specific studies for the new disciples. The objective is to help the new believer make an even stronger commitment to Christ. During these meetings, he will constantly be motivated to attend the Encounter. In this phase, the new disciple will also be screened to determine whether he has truly been converted and is qualified for the Encounter.

The Encounter's regulations, such as what to bring, departure time, and so forth, will be clarified during these meetings. The preaching of the Word during the Pre-Encounter prepares the disciple spiritually for the best Encounter with God he has ever had.

THE ENCOUNTER

The Encounter is a spiritual outing with God where one experiences what it is like to be wrapped up in His Presence. It is based on a biblical principle: a time of separation and of dying to self during a period of three days, as set forth in Hosea 6:1-3:

Come, and let us return unto the Lord: for he hath torn, and he will heal us; he hath smitten, and he will bind us up.
After two days will he revive us: in the third day he will raise us up, and we shall live in his sight.
Then shall we know, if we follow on to know the Lord: his going forth is prepared as the morning; and he shall come unto us as the rain, as the latter and former rain unto the earth.

The program and subjects for these three days are as follows:

Friday evening:
• Peniel — Seeing God Face to Face (Gen. 32:30)

Saturday:
• What Is an Encounter?
• What Does the Lord Do in the Encounter?
• Liberation
• My Behavior During the Encounter
• Amplifying Our Spiritual Being
• Inner Healing
• Going to the Cross

Sunday:
- Prayer, a Way of Life
- The New Life in Christ
- Water Baptism
- The Vision of the Church, Cells, and the Model of 12
- Baptism in the Holy Spirit

The Encounter is a time when a believer leaves behind family, work, and worries. Nothing is allowed that would distract or detract from the experience, including cell phones, laptop computers, magazines, and homework. It is a spiritual outing with a same-gender group to a place where he or she can fully concentrate on what is being taught.

Except in children's Encounters, it is very important that males are separated from females. Encounter participants need to feel completely free and uninhibited to release pain, hurts, strongholds — anything in their lives that interferes with their relationship with God. Therefore, the same-gender Encounter is a must and expands into every aspect of the three-day event. All the assistants, teachers, cooks, and so forth, are the same sex as the group being ministered to in the Encounter.

For the participants, the Encounter is an emotional ride within an atmosphere of boot-camp discipline. It is such a tremendous experience that, in some cases, the experience threatens to supercede the vision of the G-12.

In South America, almost an entire school of teaching has been developed to warn churches not to get bogged down by the power of the Encounter to change lives. The G-12 vision does not solely consist of the Encounter or consolidation; these two elements are merely a small part of the overall vision.

The Encounter is merely the beginning of great things. It is a tremendous feat, but it alone will not give you the results you're looking for. Don't make the same mistake I did of "cherry-picking" the vision — in other words, choosing the parts of the vision I wanted to implement and ignoring the parts that didn't seem necessary. I highly recommend that you implement the entire vision. Then over time, you can tailor it according to your location. It will cost you precious time if you decide to eliminate any part of the vision before you have experienced the whole of it.

In all my years of ministry, I have never experienced anything like the Encounter. It is impossible to do justice to the dynamics of the Encounter with only paper and ink; it must be experienced. Every participant promises to reveal absolutely nothing of what he has received in the Encounter, except to say that it was a tremendous experience. The fact that participants do not reveal what happens in the Encounter keeps newcomers' interest alive and the momentum going.

Although the grandness of the vision can best be experienced in churches like Bogotá or Manaus, I would like to invite you to attend an Encounter with our church in Santa Cruz, Bolivia. We can offer something few others can — an English-speaking senior pastor. On the last page of this book, you can find the information to contact us.

Everyone must experience for himself or herself what a face-to-face meeting with God can do.

OBJECTIVES OF THE ENCOUNTER

1. Dealing With the Character of the Church

God's plan is that we become equal to Jesus in character and personality (Eph. 4:11-13). His dream is to reproduce holy men of the same quality as Jesus Christ.

This is a most desirable dream. Our disciples become like us, and we become like our Pastor, Jesus Christ. We should not forget that Jesus is our Reference. This way, the earth will be full of holy people, since every healthy reproduction generates a healthy multiplication.

The Encounter deals with the character of the Church in regard to God's specific intent — the growth of every Christian into the stature of the perfect Man, Jesus. What does it mean to deal with the character of the Church? Well, first of all, the Church of the twentieth century has been tainted with many traditional concepts. The intentions of those promoting these traditions were often good, but their doctrines were wrong. False doctrine, no matter how sincere its author, harms the Church of our Lord Jesus Christ.

Second, the objectives of the Body of Christ have been distorted by materialism and the quest for creature comforts, all of which Jesus called sin. This blurring of the vision to justify sin has stopped both church growth and personal maturity.

Third, the Church entered into a very dangerous realm during the last century in which no one can be corrected without being offended. The Bible says that without correction, there is no love. It is easier to avoid offense by saying nothing and thus letting the person suffer loss on the Day of Judgment, but real love speaks the truth in love (Eph. 4:15).

The Encounter establishes a scriptural foundation on each of these points in order to put that foundation back into the local church. The goal is to restore the lost respect for leadership and the importance of working together for the common good. At every Encounter, it is stressed that God is not looking for stars; rather, He needs *lights*.

Today it is our responsibility to ask the Lord to forgive us and to turn back to our first love. We all need a deep reconciliation. We need to return to our main purpose in life — fellowship with our Father — so His desire can become ours.

God's desire is to win souls and to disciple saints. That is why Jesus died and the Church was born. If we remain faithful to biblical truths, the character of the Church will be healed, and the Body of Christ will be able to exceed its earlier exploits. Only then will the Great Commission of Matthew 28:18-20 be realized — making disciples of the Lord unto the uttermost parts of the earth.

2. Implementing the Vision With Quality

Participating in an Encounter should leave us hungry to experience more of God through the G-12 vision. How can we be satisfied with enjoying only breakfast when we know there is going to be lunch and dinner as well?

The realization of the G-12 vision is a process, and its success consists in carrying out all its steps. Therefore, do not be overly impressed with only the "set-free" anointing in the Encounter; there is still a long way to go. The cell church in the Model of 12 is an awesome project that extends far beyond the Encounter phase of the vision. God has called your church to do great things, so keep before your eyes the vision of your congregation conquering *large* territories for His Kingdom!

I want to stimulate you to be radical in this process. Go through all the phases of the vision, humbly realizing that your relationship with God can be refreshed in the Pre-Encounter, Encounter, and Post-Encounter. In so doing, you will have the right to demand it from your disciples: *"Therefore all things whatsoever ye would that men should do to you, do ye even so to them: for this is the law and the prophets"* (Matt. 7:12).

As leaders, we ourselves need to set an example in everything. First Timothy 4:2 says, *"...Be thou an example of the believers, in word, in conversation, in charity, in spirit, in faith, in purity."* We are the models. When we adhere to all the steps of the vision, we then have the right to demand the same of our disciples.

That is why it is vital that every leader goes through the Encounter himself and studies the principles of the G-12 consolidation process thoroughly before implementing the Model of 12 in his church or ministry. The vision will always be successful if it is implemented with quality.

You see, the reason the Church today is in such a poor condition is that our armies are made up of wounded soldiers. How can we be more than conquerors when we cannot even receive healing for ourselves? How could we ever hope to help others receive healing if we ourselves are still hurting? The Encounter is so very powerful because it prepares God's army for war by healing His soldiers so they can go into battle.

The Encounter is also powerful because it helps people make a commitment. Commitment has almost become a bad word in today's churches.

So don't continue to stand by the side of the road, implementing only part of the G-12 vision. Go forward, completing all the steps of the process. Conquer all its different phases. Be a model of a disciple! Your community will regard you as its representation of holy living.

3. Making the Selection

After going through the Encounter, our vision is enhanced as leaders and our ministry concepts are improved. A particular advantage of the Encounter is that it gives us the opportunity to observe prospective members of our ministry team in an extremely unique environment. This is important because, in order for the church to enter the Model of 12 cell vision, we must make a deep evaluation of the people who will be working by our side.

Choosing members for our G-12 is made easier by participating in the consolidation process. However, our selection has to be made carefully; otherwise, our personal preferences might trap us into discrediting the vision. We must ask God for guidance so the selection of the leadership and the implementation of the vision will follow all the programmed steps.

When I talk about selection, I am not telling you to cast aside the team you might already have. I am talking about the need to constantly *improve* your ministry team.

The G-12 vision is sometimes resisted because it replaces the "old guard" if they are not producing fruit. But church leaders are not mere ornaments; they must be *functional*. We cannot allow our churches to be like a Christmas tree, embellished but dead and without fruit. Therefore, the Encounter provides an even playing field from which to observe potential "fruit-producers."

Let me add this note about selecting your G-12 members: It is necessary to have great trust among your team members. All prospective members are precious, but everyone has his place and his time. A badly timed blessing often turns into a curse. Ecclesiastes 3:1 says, *"To every thing there is a season, and a time to every purpose under the heaven."* Verse 11 goes on to say, *"He hath made every thing beautiful in his time...."* Therefore, turn to God for the criteria of this selection according to the reality of your local ministry.

4. Strengthening the New Believer

This process of consolidation through the Encounter powerfully impacts the life of any believer. Any individual who has a face-to-face experience with God through the Pre-Encounter, Encounter, and Post-Encounter is changed. That person's leadership potential unfolds through the process of the vision, bearing much fruit.

That is why it is necessary to accompany the new believer throughout this process. He will be receiving a great deal of new information that is essential to his discipleship. The vision will run with quality, and the new disciple will be protected from the wiles of the devil because people are interceding on his behalf.

Besides sending the new believer to the Encounter, it is essential to place him in a Multiplication Cell in order to give him full cover. This is all part of the consolidation process and is vital to successfully passing on the vision with great patience and love.

The entire strategy of growth and multiplication depends on the vision being passed down through the descending hierarchies. Each generation ministers with confidence and ensures that its disciples do the same. The vision cannot get watered down in the process. People cannot think that former generations are better or have access to more information. As each generation gets bigger, it should get stronger according to the principle set forth in Haggai 2:9: *"The glory of this latter house shall be greater than of the former, saith the Lord of hosts: and in this place will I give peace, saith the Lord of hosts."*

Consolidation prepares the new believer for Leadership School. That is why the believer must proceed further than the Encounters. If the believer gets trapped in the Encounter phase, he'll surely abort the vision. However, if he is consolidated and gets involved in the Leadership School, the vision will be reinforced and will bear fruit (John 15:16).

In the Encounter, the vision and the process from the Pre-Encounter to the Leadership School is completely explained. Remember, the Encounter is the beginning of great things to come, but it isn't everything. Understand that the vision is only valid if the church focuses on successful cells in the Model of 12.

Stress the importance of the entire church — veteran believers and new ones — going through the Encounter. Make them aware of the fact that this is just the beginning of the journey and that there are other goals to pursue in the vision.

At the Encounter, a person receives intensive ministry in a way that challenges him. He begins to see things from the perspective of the Word of God instead of his own hurts and prejudices. The Encounter opens his heart to do exactly what God has called him to do.

As leaders, we are responsible to help people maintain an awareness of the world's desperate need for salvation and for evangelization. This awareness causes them to desire holiness as a lifestyle so they can become a greater light to the world.

For too long, the Church has been negligent, passive, and indifferent to the chaos occurring on the earth. However, the experience people receive during the Encounter and the way they become aware of their mission influences them to become disciples.

Within this entire process, participants receive enormous blessings. The awareness they experience and the conquest of territories the Lord puts into their hands brings great fulfillment. During the Encounter, people are aroused, shaken, resurrected, and stimulated to make a new start. Their spiritual sensitivity is improved, and their ability to hear God is greatly enhanced. By seeking God's will, they enlarge their house; they build additions to it; and they *grow*!

A NOTE TO CHURCH LEADERS: If we sincerely desire for our churches to conquer new territories, we must make sure we know the spiritual reality and history of our cities and discover the principalities and powers that reign in those surroundings. With this knowledge and the authority we have to step on snakes, scorpions, or any evil power, we *will* overcome!

Be strong and of a good courage: for unto this people shalt thou divide for an inheritance the land, which I sware unto their fathers to give them.
Joshua 1:6

Ask of me, and I shall give thee the heathen for thine inheritance, and the uttermost parts of the earth for thy possession.
Psalm 2:8

5. Implementing the Vision of the Cell Church Within the Model of 12

In the Encounter, participants receive a great incentive to implement the G-12 vision as they are made aware of the tremendous vision of the cell church. Everyone attending has an intense experience with the Father, the Son, and the Holy Spirit. That is why change happens so profoundly. People's horizons are widened, causing the local church to go to a new level and to experience revival.

All this is only the beginning of a long and prosperous journey. Encounter participants abandon the empty rhetoric of religion and return to their relationship with the Father. This is the Encounter's function — to become a paradigm in rejuvenating the Church as it does away with powerless traditions of the past.

6. Consolidating Both the New Believer And the Veteran Believer

Consolidation is the heart of multiplication and the foundation on which the vision rests. The vision then intensifies in the Leadership School.

Consolidation helps make new believers feel like part of something special. Our relationships with new believers and the forming of cells make us more proficient in the process of winning souls and establishing them in the Kingdom.

It's time to engage the whole church body in this vision, veterans as well as new believers. No one is to be left out; all are to be productive! The entire community will be so much healthier when all are committed to the vision.

7. Benefits of the Encounter

Everyone has a tremendous experience in the Encounter, and many have supernatural testimonies. As Job 37:5 says, "*God thundereth marvelously with his voice; great things doeth he, which we cannot comprehend.*" After the Encounter, we have new believers who are ready for discipleship, ready for the multiplication anointing (Matt. 13:23), and ready to take on the circumstances of the world victoriously.

The new believers exit the Encounter free from any ties that would keep them from growing and becoming engaged in the ministry and bearing fruit. They leave liberated from generational curses, emotional scars, and bondage to vices. All those things dissolve during the Encounter by the anointing that destroys yokes and strongholds in the Name of Jesus. Internally healed, the new believer experiences the freedom to grow and bear fruit in abundance.

It is almost disheartening to see how strongly Jesus' Church has been caught up in the bad experiences of the past. A tremendous anointing is available to heal believers from those things that have previously held them back. Luke 4:18 says Jesus came to heal the brokenhearted. His Word is the cure for all that ails us.

For the most part, everyone is completely consolidated during the Encounter. They come to comprehend God's vision for the Church and, thus, for their life. Only after the Encounter will the consolidated believer be ready to enter the Leadership School as a disciple with the purpose of serving Jesus.

POST-ENCOUNTER

Men and women can attend these meetings together. The Post-Encounter is subdivided into four meetings once a week for exactly one hour (the same procedure as for the Pre-Encounter). The subjects for the sessions are the following:

- The Importance of the Post-Encounter
- Liberation and Inner Healing
- The Areas of the Counter-Attack
- How To Resist Satan

The Post-Encounter teaches the new believer to stay alert for the devil's counter-attack, which normally takes place through worldly friendships, sinful encounters, family members, and financial struggles. At these Post-Encounter meetings, specific teachings are given on how to defend against Satan's counter-attacks, how to remain liberated, how to become strong in the

Lord, and how to fellowship with brothers and sisters in the Lord (Eph. 6:10-12). The new believer learns that by confessing his sin and by sincerely repenting and maintaining a godly attitude, he resists the devil. This crucial knowledge prepares the disciple for Leadership School.

When the Post-Encounter is completed, the believer's journey through the Consolidation process has ended.

Disciple
Chapter 4

Jesus invoked sound leadership principles by choosing this particular way to build His Church. Discipleship is little more than leadership training with a tutor. I have applied Jesus' basic principles to the G-12 vision as follows:

Five Steps to True Leadership

LEVEL 1: POSITION
(SALVATION, OR THE 'CALLED OUT' STAGE)

Each and every person has a special call of God on his or her life. Each one is necessary to complete the corporate Body of Christ because each plays a part. There are no "Plan B" personalities. God does not have someone waiting in the wings to fill in a gap in the event that someone fails. I used to think that He did because I would often hear people say, "Well if I don't do it, someone else will." But that isn't necessarily true! If someone doesn't fulfill what God has called him or her to do, it could leave a breach in the wall. Resources that were needed in one place might have to go somewhere else.

For instance, if you are called to go to North Africa as a missionary, that means a group of people is waiting for you there so they can receive Christ. If you don't go, how will they hear (Rom. 10:14,15)? That is what the Bible means when it says, *"For the gifts and calling of God are without repentance"* (Rom. 11:29). You can't repent for not fulfilling your call once you are in Heaven. In other words, you can't escape the eternal consequences of not fulfilling your call or for not using your God-given gifts while here on this earth.

The reason is this: Once you are in Heaven, there is no more opportunity to fulfill your divine call (John 9:4, 5). Your works on this earth will be judged and rewarded (Matt. 16:27). If you were called to preach the Gospel in North Africa but didn't do it, Jesus can't say, "Well that's all right. All is forgiven; here is your palace anyway." I'm sorry, but that is not biblical.

Jesus will walk you over to the gulf that divides Heaven and hell, and He will show you why He can't pardon your rebellion (Isa. 66:24). He will show you why you suffered loss of reward. He will show you your fruit — lost children burning in hell. He can't pardon your rebellion because He can't deliver them from hell and its torment. It sounds tough, but that is why it is called "the great and terrible day of the Lord" (Joel 2:11).

God is a just Judge, and He doesn't "send" anyone to hell because of someone else's disobedience. But suppose He wants you to tell someone about Jesus and you don't; as a result, that person ends up in hell. There can surely be no reward in that. God rewards according to your deeds in obedience to His will. Souls in Heaven are the fruit of your life here on earth. Less fruit on earth means less reward in Heaven (2 Cor. 3:11-15).

You are called to do something, and if you don't do it, you will suffer loss of reward for all eternity (1 Cor. 3:11-15; Heb. 12:16, 17). You will not lose your salvation, but disobedience will cost you when the rewards are being passed out in Heaven.

The moment of salvation exposes new believers to their divine call so that they are no longer ignorant of God's plan for their lives. If that is not true, then Jesus lied when He said His sheep would hear His voice (John 10:1-10).

Thus, one benefit of salvation that a new believer receives is illumination regarding the plan God has for his life (Phil. 2:12). Now that believer must begin to walk out his salvation so he might finish his course. However, the only power he has at this level is the corporate anointing, which comes from the Body of Christ as a whole. That is why it is so very important that the new creature in Christ remain faithful to church and learn to submit to authority right away before any bad habits form. The superior way to accomplish that is through consolidation and participation in a cell group.

Many people get stuck in this "saved" position. They get used to participating in the corporate anointing and never develop any authority of their own. They may try to exert authority they don't have by saying things like, "You have to do what I say because…" or "If you don't do what I say, I'm going to tell." As childish as it sounds, it happens every day among new believers. They assume a position of authority they have not yet earned in the church and then think people should follow them. Leaders operating at this level often lead by intimidation.

People resist being told what to do by someone with whom they have no relationship. Leadership is simply the ability to influence people. Titles won't move people, but a good leader's influence in their lives will.

The quality that influences people the most is a leader's personal relationship with God, not his ability to manipulate them. Manipulative tactics are worldly, and there is no profit in the flesh. If a leader has a relationship with God, the light God pours in that leader will be poured out to others. When that happens, people will notice.

But all this takes time. In order for a believer to bear fruit and give light to others, prayer, fasting, worship, meditation, study, and giving must first all be in place. Believers are called *disciples* because they are disciplined followers who obey the truth. Therefore, until all these qualities of a disciplined follower of

Christ find their place in a believer's life, he will continue to operate in the corporate anointing and not his own.

LEVEL 2: PERMISSION
(CONSOLIDATION, OR THE PERSONAL RELATIONSHIP STAGE)

The second step to real leadership is so vital because it not only allows a believer to establish a relationship with a group of peers, but it also allows the group to develop a relationship with *him*. Unlike the first level, where a leader rules by decree, a leader at this level has the permission of his followers to be their leader.

The second step is the one most people don't like because it requires dying to self. That is why they remain stuck in the "title only" position their entire lives and never really develop any power of their own.

This second step is one of the most critical, because if we don't learn to die to self, we can never really love other people. We will always be looking out for "number one" and living a selfish and miserable life. If we wish to grow beyond the simple "I'm saved" stage, we must learn how to develop personal relationships.

The Encounter part of the consolidation process is the avenue through which our selfishness is stripped away and self-confidence is given. Now, we often hear from leadership that getting too familiar with our people is bad. But if that were true, Jesus was not a good leader. Just think how familiar the disciples were with Him after living together with Him for more than three years!

Therefore, when you hear someone say too much familiarity is bad, you can know that either they have received bad teaching or there is something in their lives they don't want others to know about. The truth is, we need to be closer to each other in order to eliminate any place the devil might gain in our lives.

What I am talking about here is trusting others with one's emotions. Most people are so damaged, so beaten down, and so emotionally impoverished that the thought of their being "exposed" is almost overwhelming to them. The thought of letting others into their lives produces the same response as the thought of having their teeth drilled!

That is why we are so often cowardly, self-conscious, and unassertive in our interactions with others. We are afraid of getting hurt. Establishing ourselves in a cell group challenges and changes all of that, and, in the process, builds confidence.

When a believer allows a group to get close to him, as Jesus did, he establishes absolutes about his character as a man of God. If a group of 12 in an American court can establish guilt or innocence beyond a reasonable doubt, a group of 12 can do the same for a prospective minister of the Gospel. The multitude doesn't need to know that person personally if he has a jury of 12 who say he is okay! Thus, when a believer allows a group to hold him accountable, he is protected from demonic temptations that could rob him of his fruit or even his life.

The same is true for you as a church leader. The Bible calls you a living epistle. People can't know you from across the street. To know you, they must become intimate with you and fellowship with you. Therefore, when you establish a close personal relationship with a group you have selected, you are able to grow and to go on to the next step in the leadership process.

This is so vital. Without this group of peers to judge you and stand up for you before the masses, you have no platform to stand on. Therefore, you must allow a selected group of loyal and faithful believers to get close enough to you so they can speak for you in those back room meetings that tear leadership down, destroy pastors, and divide churches.

"Leadership" is another word for influence. Leaders are who they are because they have influenced the lives of others. Without personal relationships, leadership becomes dictatorship.

So make sure every member of your church joins a Multiplication Cell and gets involved with the group. Teach them to work hard on their communication skills and to become a servant to the group. Then they can look forward to the day when they will be trusted to lead their own cell.

LEVEL 3: PRODUCTION
(CELL LEADERSHIP, OR THE FRUIT-BEARING STAGE)

Step 3 in real leadership is the fruit-bearing stage. It is the realization of a cell member's goal to become a leader. This is the "results" level. Experience and fellowship from Level 1 and 2 result in the fruit at this level.

In step 2, the believer's goal to love others in close relationship produces true admiration in his followers as they see him accomplishing his vision. This admiration greatly enhances his confidence and influence, not with his immediate peers but with those who are more distant from him. Greater influence means greater leadership ability.

At this stage of the believer's life, solutions come easier. Cooperation from others and the availability of resources seem to just happen. As fulfilling as this stage may be, however, it is only the middle of the vision; two more steps still remain on the way to finishing his race.

Leading a cell group was a giant step in my growth, as it is in any believer's life. Leading a group at this stage is so very challenging because some of the believer's peers will be only a chapter behind him in growth. It is very challenging to stay faithful in this position because opportunities always arise to take offense or to take a shortcut by not studying, fasting, or praying.

When a believer takes on a Multiplication Cell of his own, it is his first real step toward leadership. For the first time, he is bearing fruit and fulfilling the commandment of Christ by producing disciples. His goal as a Multiplication Cell group leader is to motivate others to follow his course. He will continue to grow as he continues to serve.

LEVEL 4: PEOPLE DEVELOPMENT
(G-12 LEADERSHIP, OR DEVELOPMENT OF OTHERS)

The fourth step in achieving real leadership occurs once the admiration a new leader receives from his followers turns into faithfulness. At this point, he is in a position to help these followers develop.

At Step 3, this new leader is producing fruit in his own life, and those around him have been edified enough to want what he has. Step 4 becomes a natural outgrowth of this success if he allows it to happen by staying humble.

You can see that this is not an overnight process. Jesus' character was so strong, and His leadership was perfect. Much of what He was able to do in a few years would take someone a lifetime to accomplish! However, if the new leader's goals are consistent with the Word of God, if his desire is to be a servant and not to be served, and if he is capable of loving others no matter what the personal cost — then he, too, will grow quickly.

Some people get so puffed up and corrupted by the little authority they have that they can never go on to become a true leader. That is why so many never grow beyond their title.

This stage of a believer's life is a wonderful fulfillment of that very thing — true leadership. It is a goal few people ever really reach.

As a G-12 leader, the believer is in a position in life where he can help lift people out of defeat and help them grow like he did — first, by learning how to trust; second, how to mentor others in personal relationships; third, how to handle personal success; and, finally, how to utilize that success to benefit others.

The G-12 leader will be able to measure his success by the success of his disciples. As they grow in leadership — their cells growing and prospering — he will become more powerful. If they are doing great exploits for God, it is because they had a good example to learn from — their leader. Thus, the G-12 leader should always desire more for his disciples than what he has achieved for himself (John 14:12).

LEVEL 5: FATHERHOOD
(G-144 AND G-1728, OR THE 'SPIRITUAL FATHER' STAGE)

The respect and admiration that every father should receive is the final platform of leadership. First Corinthians 4:15 says, *"For though ye have ten thousand instructors in Christ, yet have ye not many fathers: for in Christ Jesus I have begotten you through the gospel."* Step 5 is where everyone wants to be, but very few ever get there.

At this point in the leader's life, he is greatly respected by others and exerts enormous influence in their lives. The leader knows when he is a spiritual father because he has sons — and they are experiencing greater victories than he has experienced!

Once this leader has disciples discipling disciples, he is influencing hundreds of lives and moving toward thousands. As the leader of a G-144, he will not only have between 14 and 144 G-12 leaders under his influence, but he will also have many more Multiplication Cells and hundreds of new converts.

Leading a G-1728 puts the leader in front of an army of G-12 and Multiplication Cell leaders with thousands of developing Christians in his shadow. He will have his own Encounter team and Leadership School. He will be leading a group large enough to topple small nations!

At this stage of leadership, the leader is to look to the Heavenly Father as his Example. We call our God "Father" because of His position in the universe, not because He fathered Jesus or the Holy Spirit. We call Him Father because He has total authority and all integrity.

Similarly, a spiritual father figure is one who has other successful people looking for him. He is one who is beyond reproach. His integrity is gold-plated. His word is an oath.

This is the five-step process Jesus started when He selected His 12 faithful men, although He was always God and Father (Isa. 9:6). Jesus trained His disciples in this process of producing men of God who are capable of reproducing themselves.

This process that Jesus taught His 12 disciples happens so powerfully in the G-12 cell system. It puts a method to the system Jesus used. The Good Shepherd took a group of 12 common men; After consolidating and discipling these men, He sent them out to do the same. The 12 men grew together until, finally, they could do greater things than Jesus did (John 12:14).

Leadership School

Leadership School is also essential in the discipleship process. It is vital that a solid knowledge of Scripture be passed on to every disciple so he can know how to defend his faith in love (Phil. 1:17). Great personal relationships without knowledge of the Word will produce little more than a social club.

The Leadership School is part of the church's vision and is another way to carry out discipleship efficiently. In the Leadership School, the disciples will have opportunities to steady their steps in walking with Jesus. They must grow in faith in order to be productive. The combination of the Leadership School working parallel with the character development in the G-12 is extremely effective. It sounds like an intense commitment of time and effort, and it is. But if it is important to the student, he will make the time.

There are multimillionaires, heads of states, and other very busy people involved in this program. It all boils down to a person's priorities and what is most important to him.

The Leadership School must adapt itself to the reality of the local church. However, it cannot depart from its original purpose, which is to develop new leaders.

STRUCTURE OF THE LEADERSHIP SCHOOL

G-144 leaders direct Leadership Schools. The duration is nine months, divided into three trimesters. Classes are once a week for two hours. More intense programs are also being used.

Leadership School propels the progress and growth of the vision. When the masses are pressing into the church, the frontline disciples will each be operating their own Leadership School with the help of their disciples.

When your church has Leadership Schools producing hundreds of leaders throughout the year, life as you know it will never be the same. Leadership School prepares your church to take back the spoils of the devil.

The G-12 is so powerful because it produces ministers of the Gospel, each one at the head of their own ministry. Advances are made through producing fruit, not through politics. Everyone starts from the same place; everyone has the opportunity to go all the way to the "Fatherhood" level. Directing a school of leadership is a case in point: As a leader's organization grows, he gains more and more authority. He has earned that position by demonstrating his ability to fulfill ever-greater realms of responsibility.

LEADERSHIP SCHOOL TOPICS *(9 mos.)*

First Trimester *(3 mos)*
Part One — Encounter Number 1:

- Meditation on the Bible
- The New Birth
- Advantages of the New Birth
- Growing Spiritually
- Christian Maturity
- The Baptism in Water
- The Baptism in the Holy Spirit — Part 1
- The Baptism in the Holy Spirit — Part 2
- Make Prayer a Way of Life
- The Different Types of Prayer
- The Bible: The Voice of God Today
- The Structure of the Bible

Part Two — Discipleship:

- What Is Faith?
- Different Types of Faith
- Faith Versus Hope
- Faith in Action
- Faith Versus Feelings
- What It Means To Believe From the Heart
- Confession — The Key To Loosen Your Faith
- Faith for Prosperity
- Seven Steps to Supreme Faith

Second Trimester (3 mos°)
Part One — Encounter Number 2:

- The Condition of Man
- Understanding Sin
- Classifications of Sin
- The Cross of Our Lord Jesus
- Our Redemption
- Christ Liberated Us From the Grip of the Enemy
- Opening Doors to the Enemy
- Curses: Causes and Consequences
- The Work of the Cross Brings Inner Healing
- Inner Healing
- The Cross and Prosperity
- Principles of Prosperity

Part Two — Consolidation:

- Preparing Ourselves for Consolidation
- Prayer That Overcomes
- Surrender of Our Lives to Jesus
- Distributing the Date of the Consolidation

Third Trimester $\left(3 \text{ mos.}\right)$
Part One — Encounter Number 3:

- God Seeks To Influence Our Character
- The Love of God for Humanity
- Man Was Created for God
- Understanding Our Character
- Spiritual Authority
- Spiritual Authority in the Church of Today
- Philosophies That Control the World
- Humanistic Philosophies and Christianity
- The Cults of the Last Days

Part Two — Christian Counseling:

- Christian Counseling and Its Benefits

Part Three — Homiletic Notions:

- Understanding What Homiletics Is
- How To Make an Outline for a Sermon or Message
- Different Types of Sermons

Discipleship Through the G-12

Character development is the gold the Lord is looking for in our lives. It comes from the interpersonal relationships that develop in the G-12. The long-term commitment of the G-12 has a way of bringing the dross to the top so the Holy Ghost can skim it off.

The G-12 leader holds a 90-minute to two-hour weekly meeting with his group. These meetings are compulsory because they constantly reinforce the G-12 vision. When necessary, the G-12 leader must also hold meetings with the individual members of his group. Sometimes there is no other way to resolve problems.

To *disciple* means simply to invest your life, your time, and your money into the life of another. It means to share with your disciples what you have in Christ. It means praying, fasting, and worshiping together. It means to inject your faith into your disciples — strengthening them, closing all the gaps, and destroying any strongholds the enemy might have in their lives.

We should show love to our disciples by inviting them into our homes and spending some "special time" together in the "family space" (John 1:35-39). Discipleship cannot happen through pulpit ministry because pulpit ministry is too impersonal. That is why the typical church has fewer than 120 people. It is limited in scope to the pastor's friends who perhaps inadvertently became his disciples. The non-G-12 church looks weak when compared to a G-12 church because it has no direction. It might have goals and vision, but it has no clear method to implement those goals in order to fulfill that vision.

When most pastors say they want a big church, they have no idea how to get there. They think their oratory skills will win the masses. That could happen, but only with the same likelihood as accurately betting on where lightning will strike next. And even if a pastor *could* win the masses with his ministry gift, it would rob the congregation's opportunity to do something for God other than give money to the church.

The G-12 system provides a way for the church to attain its goals in a well-organized fashion. Discipleship works through the G-12 cell group because it establishes trusting relationships between like-minded people who are working to win the world to Christ, and, at the same time, gives the satisfaction of ownership and accountability.

Re-Encounter

The Re-Encounter is an Encounter for mature saints. All the participants must be completely involved with the vision and successfully leading a G-12. In the Re-Encounter, the Holy Spirit works to heal any wounds that may have been incurred by taking on a position of leadership. The Holy Spirit also works to destroy any remnants of the past that might be holding a person back from making a commitment to the Lord.

A commitment is doing what the Lord has said; anything less is rebellion and anything more is vainglory. The path that leads to glory is narrow; the path that leads to destruction is wide.

During the Re-Encounter, the anointing pours out like a balm into the souls of the brethren because the ability to receive has been so enhanced. It's like a revision of the Leadership School and the previous Encounters, only it's much more intense. During the Re-Encounter, all the leaders are ministered to in an individual manner. The attention is doubled, and the issues are explained with greater detail and greater impact

In reality, discipleship is an eternal proposition. We are eternally in discipleship, always learning, growing and moving forward in God. However, the Re-Encounter ends the discipleship pillar in the G-12 model. The disciple is now ready to be "sent." This is the ultimate pillar of the vision.

Send
Chapter 5

What does it mean to say a disciple is ready to be "sent"? In the G-12 model, the answer is simple. When a G-12 leader gives a disciple permission to start a G-12 group, he has just sent that person out in the name of the Lord.

The Senders

The sender has a great responsibility to the congregation, because the sent one will not only be going out in Jesus' Name but in the name of the church as well.

The church, as an institution of God, stands behind the sent one. The criteria for qualifying to be sent will depend on the doctrine of your church. Be sure, however, that one of the requirements is faithfulness to the leadership and the vision.

Before a G-12 leader gives permission to anyone to launch his or her own G-12, he should first counsel with his G-12 leader. It should be handled as a nomination rather than an appointment. If the G-12 leader receives permission from his leader, he may release the new leader to begin a G-12.

The Sent

Only when all the processes of the vision have been completed will the fruit be ripe enough to pick. There are three pillars of the vision:

1. Won to Christ.
2. Consolidated into the body.
3. Discipled into a leader.

Once the leader has completed the vision, he is qualified to be sent. This means his commitment to the Lord is rock solid and sure. It also means he has completed the Pre-Encounter, Encounter, Post-Encounter, Leadership School, and Re-Encounter and, at this point, is successfully leading a Multiplication Cell. Finally, it means he is a faithful disciple to another G-12 leader.

Understanding the dynamics of Heaven should make everyone want to be a sent one — in other words, a servant to God and man. But the fact is, few are willing to pay the price. That is why a "sent one" is so valuable and so scarce.

To be trusted to begin something new is a great honor. To be sent to start a new work is the highest calling in the Bible. It means that the sender has given the sent one great authority. This responsibility must be well understood, because with that authority comes great responsibility.

The attention and power that goes along with fathering a work has destroyed many a minister. Paul said that he didn't abuse the trust he had been given when God called him to be an apostle. So, you see, when one is released to begin a G-12, great responsibility accompanies that new assignment. Eternal lives are in the new leader's hands.

Who is sent? Only those who have shown themselves worthy and who have been faithful with their time and money. Sent ones have God's motives, not selfish ambition in their hearts.

RESPONSIBILITIES OF THE SENT ONE

Being sent is a great honor because it means that a leader starts his own G-12, sets up his own Encounter team, and starts his own Leadership School. Being sent means taking new territory for the Lord.

The reason permission to start a G-12 is so important is that it includes permission to form Encounter teams, Leadership Schools, G-144s and G-1728s. It further includes sending out missionaries to duplicate the vision in other cities, states, and nations when the time comes. Receiving permission to start a G-12 is the green light needed to experience the Gospel and the fullness of leadership.

The G-12 vision is the only church-governing system I know of that actually allows and encourages apostolic gifts. It is truly an opportunity for a senior pastor to experience the joy of the Lord as he watches his disciples accomplish more than he himself did. The more successful the student is, the bigger the teacher gets. That's the beauty of it.

The goal of the G-12 is to grow into a G-144 and then into a G-1728. In order to accomplish this goal, the G-12 leader must be successful at raising a team of leaders to carry out the vision. At the same time, the team members must know that they, too, are in training for their success. From this point on, the only limit to the growth of the G-12 is the team's faith in God and their faithfulness to His Body. As Psalm 2:8 (TLB) says, "*Only ask and I will give you all the nations of the world.*"

LEADERS' ENCOUNTER

Like the Encounters before it, the Leaders' Encounter has a very special purpose. Unlike the others, it has no fixed position in the sequence of G-12 vision events. It comes about as the G-12 or G-144 leader feels it is necessary to reinforce his disciples. The goal is to bring the disciples to a realization of the cost of ministry; therefore, it is a very special time of separation and consecration.

The topics at the Leaders' Encounter are powerful and motivating. Leaders are reminded that the more they are willing to give of themselves, the greater the anointing they will have. If they want to see miracles and enjoy the Presence of God, they must pay the price.

The Leaders' Encounter usually takes place in a resort-type atmosphere versus the more Spartan setting of the other Encounters. It honors those in leadership and recognizes them for their sacrifices of love.

A Timeline Of Success
Chapter 6

The purpose of this chapter is to summarize in a personal way how the G-12 cell system works. I want to take you to a successful G-12 cell church so you can experience G-12 at its finest. To facilitate the journey, you need to imagine a non-believer struggling with a troubled marriage. (He has just recently separated from his wife.) The man attends the cell church for the first time on New Year's Day.

This is based on a true story. The names have been changed to protect the personal testimonies of those involved. The dates have also been changed in order to start the process at the beginning of the year, allowing an easier timeline to follow.

Allow the dynamics of this man's story to develop around you as you read.

A Visit to a G-12 Cell Church

After repeated attempts to talk to me about Jesus over the last three years, my sister was tempted to give up hope that she would ever convince me to have a relationship with God. She had never been able to convince me that Jesus is the answer. In fact, the more pressure family members put on me, the farther away it pushed me from God.

Although my sister stopped witnessing to me directly, she continued to pray for my salvation. She gave my name and story to one of the leaders of her church, who in turn gave it to one of the G-144 leaders. The G-144 leader passed it along to one of his G-12 cell leaders who led a Multiplication Cell group. In that Multiplication Cell group, a man named Walter started calling out my name in prayer every day. Walter spoke the Word over me for 30 days, calling me saved, healed, and whole.

This man who was praying for me was a friend of my sister. On Christmas Day, Walter invited me to attend church the following Sunday, which just happened to be New Year's Day. Before I realized what I was doing, I answered yes. He offered to pick me up Sunday morning at 9:00, and I agreed.

Sunday morning, January 1 (the day of salvation): As I drove up to the football stadium where the church services were held, I saw people rushing into a large 20,000-seat coliseum. Everyone seemed to be excited. Entire families walked toward the entrance, Bibles in hand. I didn't know what was happening, but the excitement of the people around me started to rub off on me. Anxiety about meeting God started giving way to curiosity and a desire to find out what was going on inside.

Arriving just before the service began, Walter and I walked through an ocean of people into the coliseum. Quite to my surprise, I saw several people I knew: the women who worked in the hardware store near my home, several people from my son's school, and a man I met earlier in the week selling insurance.

Once inside, the two of us found a seat. No sooner had we gotten comfortable than the band on a large platform in the end zone of the stadium started to play music. Although I didn't know any of the songs, the music was powerful and contemporary. The band started off playing fast music but then played some slower songs.

I thought to myself, *It's fun watching all the people dance and shout, but I'm very uncomfortable with people crying and raising their hands. That is exactly what I didn't want to be around. It is just too intimate for me.*

The message the pastor gave was relevant and spoke to my heart. Several times during his sermon, he mentioned something called "a cell group." At the end of his message, he invited everyone to accept Jesus as his or her Lord and Savior. He then asked everyone to say what he called "a prayer of deliverance." After the prayer, the pastor invited those who prayed the prayer of deliverance for the first time to come down to the front to be prayed for again.

The service had been like nothing I had ever experienced. The words of the pastor seemed to be targeted straight at me. Desperation had been welling up inside me during the pastor's message, so when he gave his invitation, my desire to move toward the front was overwhelming.

Without looking around or caring what others thought, I started my long walk of reflection to the front of the stadium. Hundreds of others were leaving their seats and walking in the same direction I was — toward the pastor. Once we were all gathered in front of the platform, everyone prayed a second time for salvation.

The pastor invited all the people who had come forward to follow a man with a large flag to a large hall outside the stadium. There we were met by a very large group of counselors. There was a counselor for each new convert.

My counselor asked me, "Is Jesus in your heart?"

I responded, "I think so."

"Then let's pray again," my counselor said.

Because I saw almost everyone else praying, I prayed again. I found out later that everyone prayed at least three times for salvation. I and the counselor prayed together two more times until I realized that the place where Jesus now lived was in my heart.

It was during this time that I was invited to something called an "Encounter." The counselor explained this Encounter as a "meeting with God." To prepare me for the Encounter, the counselor advised me to sign up for the "Pre-Encounter," which would begin the following Saturday.

After the eventful service, Walter explained to me that what I had just experienced was called a Celebration Service. He said that thousands of cell groups just like the one we had attended come together every Sunday to worship Jesus and to learn more about the Word of God."

Saturday afternoon, January 7 (Pre-Encounter): My sister's friend Walter, who was fast becoming *my* friend, picked me up for my first Pre-Encounter meeting. He said he wanted to make sure I didn't get lost, but I knew that Walter thought I would chicken out and change my mind. The truth was, I had thought of a million things I needed to do instead of attend the Pre-Encounter meeting. But I didn't think Walter would accept any of those things as legitimate excuses, so I had resigned myself to going to the meeting.

When Walter and I arrived at the Pre-Encounter, he sat in the back while I sat up front with the rest of the new converts. I found out later that Walter and the others in the back of the room were praying for me and the other new believers during the entire meeting.

Walter's G-12 leader was teaching the class, explaining what the results of sin. I found the concept a bit difficult to understand.

Thursday night, January 12 (first Multiplication Cell meeting): The following week, I started attending Walter's Multiplication Cell meeting in the home of one of the counselors I had met on that eventful Sunday. I couldn't help but notice that the group included only men. When I asked the group leader why, he explained to me that each Multiplication Cell group has a different vision, and his group's vision was for men. I found out later that the different "visions" are grouped into "Ministry Networks." The leader went on to explain that because my wife and I were separated, the cell group leadership thought it best for me to attend a men-only group.

Saturday afternoon, January 14 and 28 (the Pre-Encounter): For the next three weeks, I continued to attend the church services held in the stadium. However, I found that I especially enjoyed the Thursday night group meeting with other men. (Other groups met at different times during the week.)

At the Thursday night meeting, I and the other men talked about a lot of subjects — especially about what was going on in the Pre-Encounter meetings we attended on Saturday afternoons. The fun and fellowship I enjoyed in these small group meetings wasn't present in the Pre-Encounter. The atmosphere there was a lot more serious. Each week a different theme was taught, preparing us for what the leader so enthusiastically called "the Encounter." His testimony about what the Encounter did for him kept everyone coming each week in preparation for the big event.

Friday afternoon, February 3 (first day of the Encounter): Finally, it was the weekend of the Encounter. We left on a bus at 6:30 Friday evening and arrived at a ranch house at about 8:00. We prayed all the way there.

In all, there were 38 men present at the Encounter. I heard from the leaders that no more than 50 people are allowed to attend an Encounter. The object is to keep the group small enough so that each person attending can receive personal counseling.

As soon as we arrived, we made up our beds and then gathered together in a large room. The tone of the Encounter quickly became serious as the leader explained the rules. Afterward, the leader talked to the group about "'Peniel' — Seeing God Face to Face."

Saturday, February 4 (second day of the Encounter): The next morning, I and the other men got up at 6:30 so we could get to the first meeting by 7:30. It reminded me a little of my boot camp experience years ago. We had three meetings that morning; then they gave us a two-and-a-half-hour lunch break so we could take a nap. We had two more sessions in the afternoon, followed by dinner. After dinner, we had another session and then went to bed.

Sunday, February 5 (last day of the Encounter): I had started off in my new Christian walk thinking that my wife would have to give me another chance now that I was religious. I was feeling pretty proud of myself for all the things I had recently changed in my life. But by the time Sunday morning rolled around, I was feeling like a wreck. I didn't feel religious at all. In fact, I felt like the most messed-up guy on the planet!

I was wondering, *How could God — much less, my wife! — love a guy like me? How could my wife have ever put up with me? No wonder she left!*

I also found out that all the time I thought I was hiding from God, I was only hiding from myself. I never listened to my sister or anyone else who tried to talk to me about God because I didn't want to face my own selfishness, pride, or stupid arrogance. The mercy of God spent on a sinner such as me was beyond my comprehension.

Then on Sunday morning after breakfast, we had a meeting I'll never forget. It was rough. Every word the leader said cut a little deeper. He was not trying to be mean, but the truth hurt. He talked about the differences between a man and a woman and what a godly wife wanted from a godly husband. He told us things I had never heard before nor had ever really cared about.

At the end of the session, the leader helped us write love letters to our wives. (There were three other men in the group who were also separated from their wives.) It was fun writing an old-time, gushy love letter. It really gave me hope of getting back together with my wife.

That Sunday afternoon, we had a powerful session on spiritual warfare. It really charged us all up to know that we could defend ourselves against the devil. I personally went from depression to a deep sense of victory as I came to understand that Jesus had paid the price for my sin.

It was a long bus ride home. Most of the men used it to finish their letters to their wives. My letter was six pages long. I used the first two pages to ask my wife to forgive me for every offense and hurt I could remember. The other four pages expressed how much I missed and loved her. I spent the last hour trying to hold back the tears. I felt so badly about the ungodly way I had treated my wife. I was praying for a miracle.

Then the bus arrived. Hanging outside the building was a big banner welcoming us back. It was really special. The other men's wives were all waving signs with their names on them. Some of the kids were waving signs as well. The wives and children were so excited as they welcomed home their men.

I was hoping my wife would be there, too, but she wasn't. I was happy to see that the wife of one of the other guys, who had left her husband about four months earlier, was there to meet him. We finally made it inside, and the leader asked us to sit down so some of the men could give their testimonies. The wives read their letters while the men gave their testimonies.

Two of the men really stuck in my mind. The first was at least 70 years old. During the Encounter, it looked like he dropped 20 years in age. He was just bubbling with life. He was almost screaming as he told everyone what a rotten husband he had been, but he said he was going to make it up to his wife. "Praise God, it's never too late!" he exclaimed.

The other man who really got to me was closer to my age. This man came to the Encounter looking very confident and successful. But when he grabbed the microphone, all he could do was cry. His cute little wife was neatly tucked under his arm. The most he could choke out was "I'm sorry." He had told me Friday on the bus that he had lost his temper many times with his wife. The leadership just let him weep in repentance for several minutes before relieving him of the microphone.

After the meeting, I got into my car and headed straight to the post office to mail my letter.

Saturday afternoon, February 11 (Post-Encounter): The following week started what the leadership called the "Post-Encounter." These weekly meetings lasted for another month. At the Post-Encounter, we primarily talked about all that had gone on during the Encounter. My group leader reinforced everything we had been taught during the Encounter, making sure we not only understood everything but were applying it to our lives.

The last week of the Post-Encounter, the leader really honed in on what Christian fellowship, or "consolidation," was all about. He told us that without it, we would probably drift back into the world. It made a lot of sense. He talked about sheep living in flocks and said that if we would flock together, we could overcome the attacks of the "wolf." We each made a commitment to stay faithful to God, to the pastor, and to the others in our group.

After our last Post-Encounter, the cell group changed a bit. One man started going to a couples' group that he could attend with his wife. Another went to a children's group with *his* wife. The rest of us stayed in the men's group.

Saturday afternoon, March 11 (nine months of Leadership School begins): The week after I finished the Post-Encounter, the cell group leadership placed me in Leadership School. I could hardly believe it. I had only gotten saved a little over two months before, and I was already in leadership training! Things were really changing fast. My wife was talking to me again; my son liked me; and I was even doing better at work.

Six weeks after my Encounter, my wife went on a women's Encounter. Two weeks later, she moved back home. I promised to stay in church and to be more considerate of her needs.

Two months later, I asked for and received my G-12 leader's permission to start my own cell group. I asked five of my old running buddies over for a little backyard barbecue. (I had not seen them very much since New Year's Day. They had kidded me a lot about "getting religion," so I found myself avoiding them.)

The barbecue was a way to get them into my house so I could really explain what had happened to me. Once we were all together again, it seemed almost like the old days, except I wasn't drinking any beer. I didn't understand how much I had changed until I heard my old buddies talking. Then I realized, *We have almost nothing in common anymore!*

My friends were still talking about girls, dope, getting drunk, and wrecking their cars. All I wanted to talk about was Jesus. Even though I tried to get into the conversation, it was as if I was from another country. I tried to act like I was so busy cooking that I didn't have much time to talk. When I did try to share what was going on in my life, it just didn't fit with what they were talking about.

My wife, who had never liked my friends, was being so nice to them that they asked me what was up with "the old lady." Finally, I had my chance!

I started talking, and my friends started listening. I explained that both my wife and I had had encounters with God and that it had changed both of us enough to make us want to give our marriage another shot. I said, "God changed my wife so much, she even wants to help you guys out!"

Everyone was listening except one guy. All he could do was argue and ask dumb questions that were really distracting me, so I let it go and quit talking about the Lord. After that conversation, I just enjoyed a nice day in the backyard with some old friends and found out whom I could invite to my first cell meeting.

Tuesday night, April 18 (start of a Multiplication Cell): It was great! There I was, in charge of my own Multiplication Cell group. A friend from church and my four friends who listened at the barbecue were all in my house. It went really well. During the cell group meeting, one of my friends asked me, "Do we have to become religious fanatics like you to have a relationship with God?"

I was curious as to why these friends thought I was a religious fanatic. They responded, "Because you go to church every Sunday, attend a cell meeting every Thursday, Leadership

School every Saturday, and now you're meeting with us every Tuesday night. Don't you think that's a bit fanatic?"

I laughed and said, "I used to stay out every Friday and Saturday until 3:00 or 4:00 in the morning, spending my whole paycheck at the bar; watch Monday night football at John's house, staying till after midnight; play poker every week at Larry's house; and smoke dope with at least one of you guys three or four times a week during lunch. But now you say I'm a fanatic because I have a healthy family life and a relationship with God?

"No, I'm not a fanatic, and you don't have to be either. Do you really think you could spend *too much time* with God? Besides, I was so goofed up before I got saved that I need to spend extra time with God right now. My family and I turn our times with God and other believers into family fun. Is that bad?" I asked.

Tuesday nights became really exciting. Men from work started coming, and my old drinking buddies brought some of their friends. Even some of the men who had visited our church came to our cell group. I was so proud to be able to help other people find God and experience all the good things I had found.

Wednesday night, June 14 (first G-12 meeting): My cell group leader, a man named Bobby, visited my Multiplication Cell meeting and afterward stayed late to talk with me. That's when he asked me to become a part of his G-12 group. What an honor! Being in Bobby's G-12 meant that I would be in Kyle's G-144 and Pastor Steve's G-1728 group. It meant that I could go to special meetings held only for leaders.

All this leadership training was really helping me at work too. I was making more money than ever. Becoming part of a G-12 also meant that I could start my own G-12. It meant another meeting during the week, but I would soon be graduating from the Leadership School.

Saturday night, November 11 (graduation from Leadership School): I was more excited about this graduation than I was when I graduated from college. All my family and friends were out there to see me get the old sheepskin. My life had become so different now that it was hard to believe I was the same person. Thinking back over the year brought back a lot of memories, but none were as memorable as the day I gave my life to Jesus. What a great time that past year had been, getting to know God and getting reacquainted with my wife and son all over again!

Graduating from Leadership School also meant that my Saturdays would be free for a while. I was looking forward to spending more time with my son.

Friday afternoon, November 17 (first night of the Re-Encounter): This time was so different from my first Encounter. The first one reminded me of boot camp, this one was more like "R and R for the troops." The atmosphere was very different. We didn't need anyone to police us or to check to see if we were hiding forbidden items from the leadership. It was a great time of refreshing and encouragement.

Saturday, November 18 (second day of the Re-Encounter): During the day, I felt like a rock in a slingshot being pulled back farther and farther. I could hardly wait to get back out there and start winning souls for Jesus!

Sunday, November 19 (last day of the Re-Encounter): There had been some real hurts along the way since being saved. For me, more than anything else, being a leader had meant facing a lot of rejection and criticism without letting it get to me. It was rough when people whom I thought were my friends tore me apart. But Sunday was a day of healing and forgiveness. It was good for all of us.

After hearing the pastor share what he had gone through during his years of ministry, I realized I hadn't experienced anything. The Re-Encounter was also a special time because I had the opportunity to work a lot closer with the other leaders.

Three years later: That was three years ago. Now I have 83 G-12s operating under me with 230 Multiplication Cells — more than 2,600 people in all! I meet with my G-12 leaders every Wednesday night, and my wife and I lead a couples' G-12 group on Monday nights. Besides that, I teach in the Leadership School on Saturdays nine months a year. About three times a year, we have a couple's G-12 Leader Conference, which I also attend. Then, of course, there is church every Sunday.

I'm really busy for God, and I love it. Instead of watching the news every night, I am out working for the Lord. My business has never been better. My wife has never been happier, and my son has never been more secure. All I did was put my time in God's hands and let His priorities become my priorities. I found out that all the excuses for not having enough time were just that — excuses.

A 'Win/Win' Situation

The testimony you have just read is not a fairy tale. Many people are living similar testimonies every week, not only in Bogotá, Columbia, and Manaus, Brazil, but in my church in Santa Cruz, Bolivia, as well. It is enough to make any pastor jealous — and it can happen in your church!

Personally, what I like most about the G-12 is that it organizes the church so wonderfully and makes my job as senior pastor easy. With great leaders being trained all around me, I have more time to spend with God than ever before. Praying long hours used to be a dream; now it is a reality. My family life is also better than ever.

The beginning years of ministry seemed so tough because I never had enough time. Now I have ample time to fulfill my responsibilities, and my leaders do too. It is a win/win situation for everyone.

But more than anything, the G-12 system is a soul-winning machine. It works like a huge locomotive, driving right through the gates of hell and loading up passengers for Heaven. I have never experienced anything like it.

The successful G-12 churches of South America are extremely well organized, with loyal and dedicated leaders. They are a pastor's dreams come true.

The History Of Cells
Chapter 7

The cell concept certainly isn't new; God's own people used it during Bible times. Cells, or family units, have always been at the foundation of human society. Different cultures have different names for this concept, such as clan, troop, tribe, or family. But all these words mean one thing: *a small group bonded by a single interest.*

Moses and the Israelites

In John 4:22, Jesus stressed that *"...salvation is of the Jews."* Therefore, it is significant to note that early Jewish society had very strong family units, or clans, that formed the twelve tribes of Israel.

In Exodus 18, we see that the twelve Israelite tribes were then broken down into smaller groups for practical reasons. This happened after Jethro, Moses' father-in-law, saw Moses trying to minister to the needs of the massive group of Israelites all by himself. Jethro rebuked Moses for his ignorance. Then he advised Moses to break the tribes down into smaller groups and to place leaders over those groups so the needs of the people could be met.

And it came to pass on the morrow, that Moses sat to judge the people: and the people stood by Moses from the morning unto the evening.

And when Moses' father in law saw all that he did to the people, he said, What is this thing that thou doest to the people? why sittest thou thyself alone, and all the people stand by thee from morning unto even?

And Moses said unto his father in law, Because the people come unto me to inquire of God:

When they have a matter, they come unto me; and I judge between one and another, and I do make them know the statutes of God, and his laws.

And Moses' father in law said unto him, The thing that thou doest is not good.

Thou wilt surely wear away, both thou, and this people that is with thee: for this thing is too heavy for thee; thou art not able to perform it thyself alone.

Hearken now unto my voice, I will give thee counsel, and God shall be with thee: Be thou for the people to God-ward, that thou mayest bring the causes unto God:

And thou shalt teach them ordinances and laws, and shalt shew them the way wherein they must walk, and the work that they must do.

Moreover thou shalt provide out of all the people able men, such as fear God, men of truth, hating covetousness; and place such over them, to be rulers of thousands, and rulers of hundreds, rulers of fifties, and rulers of tens:

And let them judge the people at all seasons: and it shall be, that every great matter they shall bring unto thee, but every small matter they shall judge: so shall it be easier for thyself, and they shall bear the burden with thee.

If thou shalt do this thing, and God command thee so, then thou shalt be able to endure, and all this people shall also go to their place in peace.

So Moses hearkened to the voice of his father in law, and did all that he had said.

And Moses chose able men out of all Israel, and made them heads over the people, rulers of thousands, rulers of hundreds, rulers of fifties, and rulers of tens.

And they judged the people at all seasons: the hard causes they brought unto Moses, but every small matter they judged themselves.

And Moses let his father in law depart; and he went his way into his own land.

Exodus 18:13-27

From this passage of Scripture, you can see that the cell concept — in other words, ministry to small groups — has been the plan of God since the earliest of times.

The Early Church

Some of the greatest churches the world has ever known existed during those first centuries after Christ. One of the reasons for this fact is plainly stated in the Bible: The early believers met both in the temple and *in the homes of fellow believers* (Acts 5:42). According to Acts 2:2, on the Day of Pentecost the people weren't in the church waiting to receive the Holy Ghost — they were waiting in a house!

Let's look at what happened as this "house movement" continued:

And they, continuing daily with one accord in the temple, and breaking bread from house to house, did eat their meat with gladness and singleness of heart,
Praising God, and having favor with all the people. And the Lord added to the church daily such as should be saved.
Acts 2:46-47

Meeting in homes did not divide the church or cause disunity. It *built* the church. The temple meetings grew as the house meetings grew. Fellowship and eating together developed singleness of heart. Unity produced favor in the community, which helped to build the church.

You might wonder, *If the early Church was doing so well, what caused it all to change?* Well, in the third century, the Roman Emperor Constantine accepted Christ and made Christianity the new state religion. Thus, instead of persecution, believers experienced acceptance. Being a Christian became the status quo.

But once the Church became accepted by the world, it started to become worldly. Church meetings began to take place in abandoned pagan temples. Consequently, the Church adopted many customs and traditions of the pagan groups. In many ways, the people became the very thing they thought they were displacing.

When the Church moved from the model Jesus gave His followers to pagan temples, its growth stopped. As politics replaced humility and "self" replaced God, the Church turned inward. Eventually, the world moved into what we call the Dark Ages.

The Church is symbolized in the Bible as an eagle (Isa. 40:31). But when the Church moved out of the homes, it lost one of its wings and plummeted into darkness.

Two colossal events of this century have brought the Church out of that darkness: the reintroduction or revival of the Holy Spirit and small group meetings in people's homes. Currently, 19 of the world's 20 largest churches use different variations of the cell principle. The eagle is soaring again in the high places where she was meant to fly. With two wings and the leading of the Spirit, the Church is once again the light of the world!

The Historical Use of Cells In the Military

Through the centuries, the cell concept has been widely used to enhance the efficiency of military forces around the world. Let's look at a few examples.

CHINA

The ancient Chinese used the cell concept in war, much as nations do today in their modern-day armed forces. The Chinese broke down their army into smaller units of divisions and companies, with the smallest unit being a *squad*, or a group of 5 soldiers. When a general gave an order, it passed through the ranks until it finally reached the squad of 5.

A squad of soldiers came from the same village and knew each other well. As a matter of fact, if any one of the 5 squad members was unaccounted for after combat, all the other men in the group were executed. You can be sure that very few soldiers ended up missing in action! Each man's life was literally in the hands of the other members of their small group.

The Chinese found that the practice of breaking down their military force into these small groups greatly enhanced communication, specialization, and mobilization. It also improved morale and reinforced camaraderie.

ROME

Using a similar system to the Chinese, the Romans conquered the world with a sword the size of a kitchen knife and the concept of small groups for specialization and communication. Instead of 5-man units, however, they used 16-man units. Like the Chinese, the Romans learned from experience that it is much easier to maneuver on the field of battle if the larger force is broken down into smaller units.

MODERN MILITARY

The same techniques are used today with modern armies. The generals meet; orders are then passed along to the colonels, majors, captains, lieutenants, platoon sergeants, and so forth. The communication finally reaches all the way down to the smallest unit or squad comprised of 8 to 12 men.

Now change the picture and imagine a general issuing a command to 100,000 privates. There would be mass confusion! Unfortunately, most of today's churches look like the second model — a general preaching to the privates. Hence, these churches often suffer from a lack of vision, order, and healthy growth.

To help you understand just how efficiently cell groups work, imagine 40,000 men standing in a single line waiting for a nice hot meal. Not only would this be an enormous waste of time, but most of those men wouldn't have the opportunity to eat. The hot meal intended to nourish and revive would be cold and tasteless by the time it was their turn to receive their portion.

Now replay that scenario in your mind, but think of 4,000 leaders being given enough food for 10 men to cook for themselves. Can you imagine how much simpler that would make the entire process?

Feeding an army is a massive undertaking that happens several times a day in the field and under fire. Even in today's world of high-tech communications and modern warfare, the military still depends on the small group to accomplish everything. Depending on the task, different types of small groups are stacked together to form companies and divisions, which in turn comprise an army.

Implementing the Cell Group Concept In Your Church

Now let's talk about implementing this historical concept of the cell group within the local church. First of all, it's important to realize that transition into a cell church is a path to glory, *but it is a climb!*

In order to run with the cell group vision, church leadership must be totally convinced that it is the only way to have church. If there is a "Plan B," church leaders will always be greatly tempted to go back to "the way we did it before." Therefore, they must make a total commitment to not look back.

"Church as usual" will start to look good when the first hurdles of the cell system stand in your way. But don't allow yourself to get discouraged and give up (Heb. 10:39). Instead, move forward in faith to the high calling that Christ has placed on your life (Phil. 3:14).

Like any new thing, the cell system requires an up-front investment if you want to realize its rewards. For instance, a large computer software company recently reported that the average user only benefited from 15 percent of the program's capacity because he never took the time to learn the entire program. But a person doesn't throw out a new computer program when he experiences difficulties with it. He works with it until he figures it out.

That's the way you have to approach the task of getting your cell church off the ground. Don't give up when you encounter difficulties. Work with it, and the church will start to flow with the vision.

It is important to understand that the G-12 concept is a hybrid of all known cell systems. The G-12 has consolidated the strongest points of several different systems into one. The system in which you are investing is the best and most productive cell concept to date. Please note, however, it is the anointing and not a cell system that breaks the yoke (Isa. 10:27). Nevertheless, the cell church organizes and disciplines the local body so the anointing can move through it without restrictions.

Like the earlier military examples, larger groups broken down into smaller groups greatly enhance communication. The G-12 system greatly enhances communication within the local church, eliminating the negative and strengthening the positive. What church wouldn't benefit from that?

Many people find it hard to think of church life in terms of "cell reproduction" and "multiplication." To them, it all sounds too mechanical and cold. It isn't my desire to make this process seem cold or hard. On the contrary, I hope you might see the love of Jesus shining through these pages as we reach out to this world to save the lost — not with a shot in the dark, but with a strategy of success shown to us by Jesus.

If church were simply a matter of biology or science, a formula for church growth could be implemented that, when followed, would produce exactly the same results over and over again. But we are not dealing with biology here. We are dealing with supernatural spirit beings called humans! We have to leave the realm of science and enter into the world of art in order to more effectively implement the G-12 system in churches that come from a variety of cultural settings.

Art is different than science because it is subject to interpretation. The Word of God is not subject to private interpretation (2 Peter 1:20), but church government as it pertains to culture is. That is why church government is never really spelled out in the Bible. Jesus left us the "principle of 12" and the gifts of the Spirit to fulfill the Great Commission in the best way possible for each people group or culture.

That is why church growth is not a formula. And that is why every pastor, every church, and every minister can pursue this goal differently and still be successful, as long as they are faithful to maintain the integrity of the Word of God.

I want to stress this point again — G-12 is not a scientific formula for success. It is an art form that lends itself to being sculptured and modified to fit any cultural setting.

The Traditional '5 x 5' or 'Open Cell' Cell Structure

In order to appreciate the superior dynamics of the G-12 system, it is valuable to take a brief overview of the structure of its predecessor, the "5 x 5" or "open cell" system, which was developed in South Korea. The 5 x 5 system was designed by an American missionary and based on a multi-level marketing plan. As mentioned earlier, a variation of the 5 x 5 concept was utilized in the culture of ancient China.

In the 5 x 5 cell system, every "group of 5" cell group requires a cell *supervisor*, a position that has many different labels. The size of the cell in the 5 x 5 system varies from 5 to 25 members.

The 5 x 5 is a dividing cell system. In other words, the cell divides when it matures. Division usually takes place in 6 to 12 months. It continues to grow as the cells divide, building a pyramid in which the church executive officers are at the top and the senior pastor is the head.

The management system of the 5 x 5 cell structure has some inherent problems. One is that for all the supervision, there is little actual accountability. This system also requires a lot of paperwork.

Another problem — one that has drawn justified criticism — is that the cell group is forced to keep the meetings at "milk level." Why is this? Because the meetings are evangelistic in nature, open to anyone who wants to come. Thus, the needs of the incoming new Christians keep the group from maturing. Just as the group starts to grow into maturity, it divides, starting the process all over again. Continuous division in the 5 x 5 cell hinders the deeper spiritual growth of group members.

Despite the shortcomings of the 5 x 5 cell structure, it has indeed proven to be successful. Pastor David Yonggi Cho in Seoul, Korea, has built a church of more than half a million based on this model, so it obviously works. However, the 5 x 5 structure can present some challenges.

Structure for a Traditional 5 x 5 Cell System

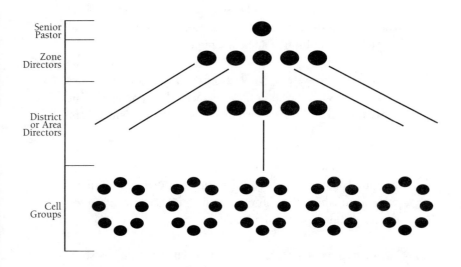

FIGURE 1

It's very important to notice the large supervisory staff needed to manage a 5 x 5 cell system. It operates almost on the Peter principle. When someone is successful as a cell leader they are taken out of that position and placed into supervision. The system then loses a proven cell pastor. This system makes for a lot of paper work and neutralizes leadership capacity.

For instance, the division of a cell can sometimes be like a lifeboat leaving the mother ship, both painful and joyful. The cell group members who have to leave the original cell group often feel abandoned or even angry. Some take offense and end up leaving the church altogether. On the other hand, cell group members who don't get along are often happy when a cell division gives them the opportunity to get away from each other.

Also, the 5 x 5 system does not allow the leadership to select the group's members. Therefore, an unrelated group of people gathering together with little or nothing in common except their neighborhood location is not necessarily a contented group. (Even though Christians are to love everyone in Christ, they don't always *like* everyone!) If people are assigned to a cell group based on geography, zip code, or some other logistical means, a split may be viewed as a relief to many of the group members. By contrast, the G-12 system is not based on *geography* but on *vision*.

On the opposite side of cell division, however, is unchecked cell growth. This situation arises when a cell *should* divide but doesn't. Instead, it just keeps growing bigger and bigger.

The problem with oversized cell groups is that they lose the original vision. They can no longer communicate according to First Corinthians 14:26:

How is it then, brethren? when ye come together, every one of you hath a psalm, hath a doctrine, hath a tongue, hath a revelation, hath an interpretation. Let all things be done unto edifying.

When a cell group grows too large, it loses its effectiveness to communicate in a personal way and turns into a Bible study or a "church plant," neither of which are its goals. There is a time to use a cell group to plant a church, but a "runaway" cell is not one of those times.

The G-12 Cell System

During the '70s and '80s, several large churches were experimenting with different forms and concepts of cells. The leaders of these churches discovered some of the same weaknesses as have already been discussed in the 5 x 5 cell system. As I mentioned previously, Mission Charismatic International in Bogotá, Columbia, pastored by Cesar and Claudia Castellano, is the church that advanced the G-12 cell system.

Pastor Cesar acknowledges that several other pastors were working with variations of the "12 x 12" concept at the same time he was. It was his superior leadership that brought what he was doing to the forefront of cell church technology.

Pastor Cesar's vision and drive were fueled by his great frustration with seeing people leave the church after he had invested himself into their lives for years. Many pastors know what it is to pour their lives into church members, only to watch them move on to another church, or worse yet, to backslide. This is one of the greatest disappointments a pastor can face.

In Pastor Cesar's case, he prayed, "God, if being a pastor means watching people leave after pouring my life into them, then I quit!"

Pastor Cesar did pull back for a season of prayer and fasting. But God wouldn't let him quit. Instead, He gave Pastor Cesar a superior way to pastor his church. The Lord took Pastor Cesar to a passage in the Bible that revealed His plan for divine multiplication, using the pattern Jesus established while ministering on earth:

And it came to pass in those days, that he went out into a
mountain to pray, and continued all night in prayer to God.
And when it was day, he called unto him his disciples: and of
them he chose twelve, whom also he named apostles;
Simon, (whom he also named Peter,) and Andrew his
brother, James and John, Philip and Bartholomew,
Matthew and Thomas, James the son of Alphaeus, and Simon
called Zelotes,
And Judas the brother of James, and Judas Iscariot, which
also was the traitor.
And he came down with them, and stood in the plain, and
the company of his disciples, and a great multitude of people
out of all Judaea and Jerusalem, and from the sea coast of
Tyre and Sidon, which came to hear him, and to be healed of
their diseases.
Luke 6:12-17

Thus, the model for multiplication that Jesus set forth was
based on a group of 12 men trained to duplicate their Leader's
efforts. The results of this original model can be seen in the
millions of souls who profess Jesus Christ as their Lord today.

Since that time, International Restoration Ministry, in Manaus,
Brazil, pastored by René de Araújo Terra Nova, has adopted
and streamlined the G-12 cell system developed in Bogotá,
making it even more effective. As mentioned in the Preface,
revelation always grows when it moves into a new culture. The
Brazilian model is much more effective at handling the
transition to the G-12 system than was the earlier Columbian
model. Pastor Araújo Terra Nova has been enormously
successful, taking his church from 6,000 to 20,000 in less than
two years.

Currently, the fastest-growing churches in the world are in
Latin America, and they are all utilizing the G-12 cell structure.
The tremendous success of these churches has the rest of the

Christian world asking themselves, "What are they doing to double their congregation every year?"

In the last few years, the Bogotá church has grown to more than 100,000 active members in cells. At last count, the young people in the congregation numbered in the thousands. The church holds weekly meetings in the local sports stadium, filling it with thousands of excited teenagers on fire for Christ. They have revival every day!

Wouldn't you like to experience this in your church? What are these churches doing to reap this kind of growth? Their vision rests on consolidation. Consolidation is what it takes to make people stick.

Due to the language barrier and the rapid growth of the churches in Columbia and Brazil, the available information on the G-12 cell system has been very limited. The ministry teams of the two churches have produced several books that help explain this cell concept and what is happening in their churches. Unfortunately, all the material has been written in Spanish or Portuguese. In addition, the writing style of the available Spanish or Portuguese literature provides more theory and testimony than a "nuts and bolts" explanation of how they are actually implementing this system.

As I mentioned earlier, I pastor a church in Santa Cruz, Bolivia. My position in the Body of Christ as a missionary to the Latin world has given me the unique opportunity to read and understand the literature of these two churches, as well as to speak with their staff about what they are doing and how they are doing it. My church has benefited so much from this information that I have taken the time to write this book so that you, too, might benefit from the G-12 cell system.

This book addresses "the Jesus way" to evangelize and build churches. Winning the lost and taking the Gospel to the ends of the earth is a divine plan. If you are tired of seeing almost as many people leave your church as come into it, it's time to discover the plan of salvation that Jesus used to establish His Kingdom on earth. God has never told us to do anything without telling us how to do it! Jesus showed us how to do it. We have failed to follow His example, however. His divine plan of salvation worked great during His earthly ministry. Imagine what it can do for you!

I have written this book in order to make available in English the information that is causing Latin American churches to explode. The American Church has been doing a great job of winning, discipling, and sending, but thousands continue to slip out of the net. Meanwhile, the vision of WIN — CONSOLIDATE — DISCIPLE — SEND is making the Church in Latin America grow faster than anywhere else in the world.

Consolidating the saints in the Body of Christ is the strongest aspect of the G-12 structure. It enables a church to close the back door. Can you imagine how large our churches would be if we could just hang on to 20 percent more of our visitors? Wow!

Why Cells?
Chapter 8

"Onward, Christian soldiers, marching off to war...." So goes the familiar old hymn. But what a mess of an outfit we are! Our "armies" are made up only of privates and generals because of lack of trust and pride. Envy and strife exist among the ranks. Gossip and rumors can be heard behind every command. Soldiers are so wounded that they can hardly stand, much less fight the good fight of faith. Those who are succeeding are being brought down by "friendly fire." For all its pomp and circumstance, for all the billions and billions of dollars spent on itself, the Church is not getting the job done.

So why is the cell system the solution to this sorry state of the Church at large? Because every local church in the world already has cells in the form of special interest groups, cliques, and business interests. If a congregation includes more than three families, it has small groups.

Thus, the question is this: Since we already have small groups within our churches, what is the best way to manage them?

Reality Check

In her book *Worship Evangelism*, Sally Morgenthaler gives us this alarming information:

"Where did all the people go? Dissatisfied customers tend to vote with their feet, and that is exactly what has started to happen in churches across the country. Church attendance is becoming increasingly erratic (half of the people who say they go to church attend only once a month or less), and in all but one sector of the population, the rate of attendance is going down. In fact, the 1994 figures for overall adult attendance were the lowest in ten years: 42 percent. That is down from 49 percent in 1991. Do the experts really know what people want when it comes to God and church in the late twentieth century?"[1]

And what about the famed Baby Boomers? A *Time* magazine cover story in 1993 reported that they were coming back to church. Are they really? There are plenty of indications that the Boomers who flocked to our mega-churches in the 80s (approximately 25 percent of the total Boomer population) are either headed for the exit signs or are already out the door. In fact, George Barna, well known for his marketing research, now lists Boomers as one of the groups having the greatest ambivalence about church attendance.

In three years, weekly Boomer church attendance dropped 11 percent. Of those Boomers who still attend services, only 33 percent attend four times a month. Twenty-eight percent attend two times or less. Incredibly, 24 percent of Boomers who consider themselves Christians now skip worship completely, with 30 percent attending only once or twice a month. These developments are particularly alarming when we consider that many mega churches have focused entirely on Boomers for the past ten years, spending disproportionate share of their resources and energy to get them back to church.

Wade Clark Roof, author of *A Generation of Seekers* and *The Spiritual Journey of the Baby Boom Generations*, says this:

"Many of the conservative returnees left mainline congregations out of disillusionment... The disillusionment is [still] widespread, which is why there is so much movement in and out of congregations to begin with. In all the searching and

[1] *Sally Morgenthaler, Worship Evangelism (Grand Rapids, Michigan: Zondervan, 1995), p. 20.*
[2] *Wade Clark Roof, A Generation of Seekers: The Spiritual Journeys of the Baby Boom Generation (San Francisco: Harper, 1993), pp. 236, 77.*

shopping around, some find what they are looking for in church, but many do not and drop out.... Just showing up and going through the motions is what many Boomers abhor about church going.... [It] can easily smack of hypocrisy to a generation that has felt estranged from social institutions and insists upon authenticity and credibility as prerequisites for commitment."[2]

Sally Morgenthaler goes on to say in her book *Worship Evangelism*:

"A recent study shows that Boomers do not consider the church more relevant as a result of all the worship changes we have made. The Boomer stampede is definitely over. They came, they saw, and many of them left.
Boomers are not the only ones who are sleeping in and reading the paper...two other adult age groups show even greater drops in church attendance. In three years weekly attendance among Busters (born approximately 1965 to 1983) fell 17 percent and among seniors (born before 1927) an unbelievable 24 percent! Mysteriously, as these declines were being charted year after year, they went largely unnoticed in church-growth circles. Even the substantial drop in Boomer attendance received only scattered acknowledgment. All together, a Gallup survey reports that 38 percent of all church-going Americans are attending church less frequently than they did five years ago."[3]

"We are producing a generation of spectators, religious onlookers lacking any memory of a true encounter with God, deprived of both the tangible sense of God's presence and the supernatural relationship their innermost spirits crave. A sickening emptiness pervades much of the born-again experience of the '90s, and the hollow rituals played out week after week in so many of our worship centers attest to it."[4]

[3]*Morgenthaler, pp. 21-22.*
[4]*Ibid., p. 17.*

"Unfortunately, many of us as pastors and church leaders are unaware that people are becoming dissatisfied, particularly in churches with attendance of a thousand or more. Our worship centers look full every Sunday. The numbers are up or at least being maintained. Yet on any given Sunday only about 50 percent of the people are returnees from the previous Sunday. Even if we are aware that our front door has now become a revolving door, we ignore the fact as long as more people seem to be coming in that are going out."[5]

Morgenthaler also quotes George Barna as saying, "We are more impressed by a church of 4,000 people who have no clue about God's character and His expectations than by a church of 100 deeply committed saints who are serving humankind in quiet but significant ways."[6] He also says, "I don't think numbers and numerical growth are most important. What I see the Scriptures telling us is that a successful church is where people's lives are being transformed and becoming more Christ-like. You'll never get a quality ministry by focusing on quantity first. Quality must precede quantity."[7]

Morgenthaler continues:

"Reaching the believer has been the evangelical battle cry of the last decade. Yet church attendance before the recent slump was virtually flat — a stagnant 45 percent of all Americans. How, then, do we explain the phenomenon of the mega-church? Simple: musical chairs or church-hopping growth. And it represents more than 80 percent of the people who have come in our doors in the past decade. That is scary. Scarier still is this future scenario painted by Bill Hull: "The mega-church's feeder system is the smaller church and disgruntled believers who have quit their churches. What is going to happen when that feeder system dries up?" What indeed? Barna predicts that a hundred thousand small churches will close their doors.

[5]Ibid., pp. 22-23.
[6]George Barna, The Barna Report 1994-1995: Virtual America (Ventura, California: Regal Books, 1994), p. 147.
[7]Morgenthaler, p. 18.

Let's take a look at American evangelical land as it heads into the next century. Here is Barna's satellite view: "We have 325,000 Protestant churches, 1,200 Christian radio stations, 300 Christian television stations, and 300 Christian colleges.... During the last 8 years, we in the Christian community have spent in excess of $250 billion in domestic ministry and have seen a 0-percent increase in the proportion of born-again adult Christians in this country. Are we concerned about this? Do we feel any accountability for this picture? Or will we continue to play the same games?"

More statistics paint an even bleaker picture: Five thousand new churches were started between 1991 and 1994, and spending for those three years alone topped $100 billion. Yet the percentage of those calling themselves born-again Christians dropped from 40 percent in 1992 to 35 percent in 1994. Again, in cost-to-benefits terms, we are not getting our dollars' worth!

Compare the American outreach scenario with the impressive Kingdom gains in places such as Africa, Latin America, and Eastern Europe, and with worldwide conversion rates. The U.S. Center for World Mission tells us that the number of Bible-believing Christians — those who are seriously Christian — has risen from 6.2 percent of the total world population to 9.9 percent just since 1980. In the same period of time, evangelical churches in Latin America grew in membership from 18.6 million to more than 59 million.[8]

As you can see, Latin America is way ahead of the pack!

What is the solution? It can't be more money. The American Church spends billions of dollars every year. As a matter of fact, according to World Vision, eight out of every ten Christian dollars are in America. The solution also can't be better marketing. A big chunk of those billions are going to state-of-

[8]*Ibid., pp. 26-27.*

the-art mass media communications. Better sound systems or better music can't be the solution. Only professional recording studios using professional artists rival the worship in American churches. A church's excuse can't be that it is restricted by the size of its building. On the contrary, many churches have huge buildings that are not being filled, much less filled to overflowing.

We can all agree with Sally Morgenthaler when she says, "People make time for what is important. People today are value-oriented."[9] That makes me wonder what kind of message we are putting out as the Church, if worshiping and spending time with the Father is no longer perceived as valuable or important!

What Is the Solution?

What is the solution to this decreasing interest in the local church among Americans? Well, let me answer that question with another question.

Have you ever wondered why there were only 120 people waiting in the Upper Room to receive the power of the Holy Ghost? What happened to all those who had received healing miracles? How about the thousands who had received food? How about the 500 who saw Him ascend into Heaven? Why were there only 120 in the Upper Room?

The answer is there wasn't enough room for more! The Upper Room was not too small. The apostles weren't restricted by the size of the room, but by relationships.

If the remaining 11 apostles were operating according to what Jesus had taught, they were each working with a small group of disciples. Let's say each of the 11 apostles had gathered

[9]*Ibid.*, p. 23.

together 10 or 11 disciples. It is easy to see why there were 120 disciples gathered together in that Upper Room on the Day of Pentecost.

It is also easy to see that the thousands who were touched by Jesus' ministry were not added to the Church. Praise God for all the miracles, good works, and everything else. But when it got right down to it, growth was limited by personal relationships.

Lack of relationships is restricting growth in today's churches as well. Churches stop growing when they run out of space for relationships. That's why the vast majority of the world's churches operate with fewer than 120 people. Here again is that number 120. This seems to be the ceiling for the number of people who revolve around a clan made up of a pastor, his family, and a few close friends.

After Pentecost, the Church grew and expanded by the thousands. This was not because of massive crusades, the availability of huge buildings, or the coverage of mass media. The Church grew because there was enough room in relationships to absorb more people.

The disciples had spent more than three years with Jesus being trained to operate in small groups. It was this training that prepared the early Church to grow the way it did. Each new disciple added to the early Church was trained as Jesus' disciples had been trained. It doesn't take much math to figure out how fast 12 times 12 times 12 grows (12 x 12 = 144; 12 x 144 = 1,728; 12 x 1728 = 20,736). In only three generations of growth, more than 20,000 people could be added to the Church.

If we will just stick with the Bible, we'll be okay. The Word reveals that development of relationships is the key to growth.

Acts 2:46 and 5:42 say the early believers were daily in the church (temple) and in every house. Church is a great place to meet, but the home is where believers develop relationships! The early Church could grow because there was room spiritually and emotionally for the people.

The G-12 cell structure organizes the local body in such a way as to establish discipline and order. But more than anything else, it promotes holy relationships. Cell groups are the answer, and G-12 is the superior cell system, according to men of God like David Yonggi Cho, Laurence Kong, Ralph Neighbour and Pio Verkeme.

G-12 is a strong and effective system because it is not based on some foreign culture; rather, it is based on the biblical "principle of 12," meaning 12 people or couples grouped together under a single leader. Each of the G-12 members is a leader of his or her own group of 12. As mentioned before, the G-12 uses techniques similar to what Jesus used while He was on earth.

The G-12 will change your concept of the traditional church and even traditional cells. It works because it is so simple and because it succeeds so well in constantly expanding relationships without burning people out.

During a television interview, the renowned evangelist Billy Graham was once asked whether or not he would change anything if he could do it all over again in ministry. "Yes," he replied. "I would find 12 men and pour myself into them and ask them to do the same." He went on to say, "The infinite wisdom of Christ's example should have been an example for us all. The 12 that Jesus poured His life into have multiplied themselves into more than a billion."

Reverend Graham recognized the need for believers to reorganize the local church, as well as to reevaluate the way they think about evangelism according to what Jesus did while He walked this earth. Jesus picked out 12 faithful men. Later, they followed His example by doing the same. This method is straightforward and extremely effective. In the first centuries after the resurrection of Jesus, the globe was almost encircled by the Gospel on foot using this simple formula.

A Word to Pastors

Over the years a great deal of misunderstanding has existed within the Church about cells and small groups. Many think this method is a Korean or South American phenomenon not suitable for the Western world. Horror stories of church splits and other failures within cell churches have kept some from launching out into the pattern for successful multiplication that Jesus showed the Church centuries ago.

I must warn you that if you are looking for fame or stardom, this is not your ticket. Jesus' pattern for successful ministry — working with a small group — did not make Him famous in the eyes of the world. Apart from the Bible, there is almost no evidence that Jesus ever lived. No great statues were erected in His honor during His lifetime.

However, consider this: Jesus' life and ministry succeeded in establishing God's Kingdom on the earth. During the first few centuries of that Kingdom, the Gospel was preached to every house in Asia, the Middle East, and parts of Africa and Europe. The original disciples and the apostle Paul almost completed the Great Commission in the first century by using the principle of small groups.

Pastor, if you have grown weary of watching new members join your church, only to see them leave, you are ready for cell groups. If you want to close the back door of your church and stop the flow of departing church members, you need the G-12 cell system.

As a pastor, my greatest disappointment was seeing almost as many people leave the church as had come in. But cells have changed that situation in our church. The back door still exists, but it is a lot smaller. And those who do stay love the Lord, are more disciplined, and have greater joy.

As pastors, we spend thousands of dollars getting people into our churches. Then after they're born again, we turn them back out. Follow-up in most churches is little more than a house visit. On the other hand, the cell church nurtures and cares for the new Christians while they are developing. It helps defend them from those first barrages of offenses that would send them back into the secular world!

How about the families who come from other churches? Because of their past experiences, they are almost always looking for offense. Many come with a very critical attitude, ready to find out what's wrong with your church. After coming in wounded, they look for excuses to leave. The cell system will not only nurture them into recovery but will also bring them to a new place of commitment and loyalty.

Pastor, you need cells to do what you cannot do: *BE THERE!* Once your church has become larger than 20 to 50 families, there is just not enough of you to go around. That's why most churches never grow beyond 120 members. The whole structure is leaning on one person — the pastor.

Some pastors act as the sole ambassadors of Heaven in their church. They feel as though they need to speak into the lives of every family and member.

But if your church is to grow, authority must be given to others. Cells are a proven way to delegate authority. You can trust those to whom you have given authority because the G-12 system holds each one accountable.

A Word to Traveling Ministers

If you are a traveling minister and are tired of doing all the work of your ministry by yourself, develop a cell. You need a cell group because you need support, both logistically and spiritually.

Within your cell group, place a ministry team around you that can help you pray and solve administrative problems. There should also be fellow members in the group who will help you carry the load of the ministry. (Traditionally, you would call this type of cell a "Board of Directors.")

If your support cell is operating under the covering of a local church, it will bless both you and the pastor. Your ministry cell group will help stabilize the local church and give you the needed assistance. The result will be a natural process of growth for both you and the local church.

Many pastors are intimidated by ministries that operate outside their churches. They perceive these ministries as entities representing division or a threat to their authority. Pastors sometimes regard all but in-house ministries as a departure from the vision of the church.

However, if a traveling minister is the leader of a cell that represents his Board of Directors, he has the spiritual and logistical help he needs to fulfill his calling. At the same time, he helps support the local body as a whole by being an integral part of the church.

So, you see, instead of taking away from the vision of your local church, you add to it by developing your own support cell group! The cell group is the ticket to both being accepted and blessed by your pastor, as well as having your ministry needs met more effectively.

A Word to Missionaries

One of the greatest challenges for missionaries is the administrative support back home. That is why there are more than 29,000 missions agencies. These agencies endeavor to provide the missionary with administrative support back home so the missionary can be more effective in the field.

Being a missionary myself, I can tell you that the last challenge a missionary needs is a problem or a difficulty back home. The answer to this challenge is a cell group — a caring group of people whose cell vision is your mission.

As a missionary, you will find that your own mission cell can bless you beyond your imagination. It can provide the same services as a missions agency without your having to pay any surcharges. Also, instead of threatening the pastor with a competing vision, your mission cell will become a complementing element of your local church, averting the perception that you are draining resources from the local body.

Another significant point for you to note is that the G-12 system is proving itself to be extremely effective at discipling believers in so-called "closed countries." Missionaries and nationals alike whose governments have outlawed Christianity are finding that the principles in this book greatly facilitate evangelism and discipleship because the system allows expression to the Gospel without drawing attention to itself.

To the Body of Christ in General

Why do we need cells? Because cells are a way for every saint to earn his or her heavenly reward. The religious concept of ministry being performed by a priest on behalf of the laity went out long ago — all the way back when the veil in the temple was torn, exposing the Holy of Holies to all men (Matt. 27:51; Heb. 10:20).

Under the New Covenant, we are called to be a chosen generation, a royal priesthood, a holy nation, a peculiar people (1 Peter 2:9). Along with that, however, comes great responsibility. Many of Jesus' parables are in reference to the rewards earned in this life that we will be carrying over to the next one. Salvation was purchased for us with the blood of Christ, but every man must earn his own reward. To think otherwise is not scriptural.

In First Corinthians 3:10-15, Paul talks about the ultimate judgment for believers. In these verses, he talks about the loss some will suffer — an eternal loss! The idea that there are no tears in Heaven is false. The Bible says that Jesus will wipe away our tears (Rev. 7:17; 21:4). Many will suffer loss because they were not obedient to the will of God. Unfortunately, once His judgment is served, it will be impossible to repent and recover that loss (Rom. 11:29; 1 Cor. 3:10-15; Heb. 12:12-16).

Jesus is the Foundation. His sacrifice purchased your lot in Heaven, but your palace is constructed with the gold, silver, and precious stones of your obedience. Warming the pew on Sunday is probably not going to put you on Prophet Avenue, Missionary Drive, or Apostle Circle in Heaven!

We need cells so everyone can have the supernatural opportunity to earn what Jesus calls crowns and thrones in the life to come (Luke 22:30; Rev. 4:10; 20:4). One way pastors can give that opportunity to their church members is by sharing the responsibility of the ministry.

In Greek, the term "pastor" does not carry the meaning of "superman." Pastors have their families and friends just as their church members do, but too often the congregation lazily allows their pastor to spend himself, even to exhaust himself, on their needs. In contrast, cells allow the local body to function in a scriptural, healthier way, with every member of the church being fitly joined together (Eph. 4:16).

Believers within a local church need each other in order to accomplish what God has called that local body to do. The beauty of the G-12 structure is that it is a win/win situation for everyone. It's not a select few ministering to the lazy because *everyone is a leader*.

Everyone has a destiny in Christ, waiting to be discovered and fulfilled. The G-12 system is an excellent way of managing and encouraging the fulfillment of each divine destiny represented within the congregation of a local church.

Why Some Say Cells Don't Work
Chapter 9

The number-one reason why some cell churches don't work is lack of vision. This problem is described in Proverbs 29:18: *"Where there is no vision, the people perish: but he that keepeth the law, happy is he."*

Most people think small; large thinking can be too overwhelming. People say, "Cells won't work with our people." They are speaking out of ignorance because they have never tried it.

Cells can never work if you don't use them. The only way to find out if cells work in your church is to implement them wholeheartedly!

Some say cells don't work in America or in the Western world. The fact is, cells are already working in North, Central, and South America, as well as in Europe, Africa, and Asia! What these people are really saying is that, for most Westerners, a small-group Encounter is simply too intense, too personal, and too invasive for their self-centered lives.

The second reason for failure is that ministers have had the vision for small groups but not the *mechanism* for them. In other words, they had the vision, but they didn't have a clear plan of action to accomplish that vision.

Typically, visionaries are not the best administrators. The visionary sets the course, and the administrator keeps it on track because having only a *vision* for cells is not enough; the plan must be administered correctly. (By the time you've finished reading this book, you will have both a vision for growth and you will understand the mechanics of operating cells successfully in your church or organization.)

Third, cells won't work if there are rampant character flaws among the cell members. Selfish ambition and glory hounds will find little attraction to cells. Cells don't produce stars; they build the Kingdom of God. Cells require Bible-believing faith in the hereafter and in an eternal reward for being a good steward of both time and resources. Cells require dying to oneself in loving service to others.

Unfortunately, these biblical values are not Western values. Ministers looking for stardom sometimes don't like the cell concept because they don't see how it is going to promote them personally. Cells have drawn a lot of flak from this group because they see "cell success" as competition to Christian empires built to self. They don't know how cells work, and they don't want to know.

Cells threaten this group. Somehow, a spirit of demigod has entered into some of our churches. The pastor has become the owner of people's souls instead of the helper of their joy.

Others don't want to believe that cells work because they are afraid their sins will be discovered or, worse still, that their selfish ambitions will be uncovered.

You can be nice to your wife in church even if you are not talking to each other at home. But when meeting in the home, it is a different story. You might be able to fake it for a while, but sooner or later, a bad relationship will start to show up. Problems with the children will start to come to the surface. Bad money management will become obvious. All the things that are so easily hidden in the traditional church will begin to be revealed. So if you don't like the idea of cells, you should examine yourself and ask yourself why!

How many times have couples within a church divorced without anyone in the congregation even knowing they were having problems? I'm not just talking about the "wallflower couples" in the church — in other words, the regular church members who hold no position of authority and are therefore not in the spotlight. I'm talking about the pastors, deacons, and elders whose colleagues knew nothing about their marital problems until their divorce.

Unless we are in someone's home regularly, we don't know what is going on in their lives. Small groups are good because they hold us accountable.

Jesus didn't regard equality with God a thing to be grasped; rather, He humbled Himself to be held accountable by a small group (Phil. 2:6). How much more should any minister of the Gospel also fashion his ministry after Christ's example?

Jesus chose to work within the dynamics of a small group for a very good reason: He wanted to show Himself approved. He had nothing to hide. Yes, He sent out the 70, and, yes, He preached to the multitudes. But the foundation of Heaven is named after the 12 men He walked with on earth. They were His community, His cell.

Another reason some people oppose cell groups is *fear of division*. Many church leaders and pastors are afraid that cells will breed division. However, a properly organized cell church is the best defense against church division or a church split. Cells actually guard against division by organizing the church into manageable groups. They are like fire breaks in large buildings. If fire does break out, it may be contained to a small section, saving the structure at large from destruction.

Remember the story of Absalom? Many pastors have preached about the sin of Absalom in an attempt to keep division out of the church, when Absalom was actually a direct result of David's failure to restore relationships. David cried so grievously at Absalom's death because he was mourning his own failure as a father.

Division in the church is so very painful because it identifies the failure of the pastor and/or leadership to maintain proper relationships. But cells *foster* strong relationships. They also help eliminate the strife that leads to splits or divisions.

The cell church is all about relationships — maintaining and restoring spiritual sons so they will not need to revolt. Even if a wolf does get in, all he can take with him is a single small group — not the whole church!

Thus, when your church is organized into small cell groups, it is protected against a split. You minimize your losses in case of a fight.

The fact is, a pastor's fear of division fuels the very thing he is hoping to prevent. What's worse — losing 90 percent of the church people through the back door or a small group through a split? The bottom line is that people leave because they are unhappy and dissatisfied. Their needs are not being met, so what is the difference if the loss is all at once in a split or a few every week?

Thus, although some might perceive starting cells as a risk, the church is actually losing more through neglect than through rebellion!

Unfortunately, the fear of division or church split is the major reason pastors don't like cells. Let's delve into this point a little more closely. The church can be broken down into two groups: those who want to minister and those who want to be ministered to. Both groups have real needs. The first group leaves because they're frustrated at not being able to use the gifts God gave them. The second group leaves because they are not being ministered to; they need more attention. What G-12 does so very effectively is to put these two groups together to work with each other instead of against the church and the pastor.

The "potential Absalom" never appears in an environment where the needs of the people are being met. Cells properly managed are a church's best insurance against a split that occurs when needs are not being met, and against anyone leaving through the back door. The tension in the church caused by these two groups is released through the cell ministry. One person can minister while another is ministered to. They no longer need to wait three weeks to speak with the pastor about a problem; they can take it directly to their cell group or their cell leader.

As a result, the cell leader gains insight into the pastor's burdens. Instead of criticizing the pastor because he doesn't return phone calls the same day or doesn't shake everyone's hand at the service, the cell leader is faced with exactly the same situations. Dealing with people becomes his concern and, thus, the pastor gains a brother who understands him instead of an Absalom who criticizes him or tries to take his pulpit.

The reason some cells don't work is that they are not given the chance to work. Many times, cells are just another program of the church, competing against all the other programs for resources, time, and people. But in order for cells to work, they must become the focal point of the church! In other words, a cell church is not merely a church with cells.

Let me clarify this statement. In a cell church, all the other ministries grow out of relationships that are formed within the cells. The cells are the government of the church. Everything works through the cells. It is a radical change from the "good ol' boy" political system so often used in churches today. Cells have a way of showing who has the goods and who doesn't have them.

Moving from a church with cells to a cell church radically changed the church I pastor. In the switch, most of the church's leadership changed. Leaders I thought were strong were in truth only talk and no action. When it came down to who could multiply themselves through a cell group, some just couldn't make it.

You may ask, "Why was someone holding a leadership position who couldn't hold a small group together and multiply?" That is a reasonable question. It indicates the reason why cells don't always succeed in well-established churches. The churches are too well entrenched in their political systems.

The cell system promotes those who serve. It uncovers the true gifts and callings of a person. It separates the talkers from the doers.

Many fear the cell because it reveals the true ability and character of each pastor, staff member, deacon, elder, or other church leader. Fear of exposure keeps many from entering the cell concept. Some also believe that the familiarity found in a small group would breed contempt for those in leadership.

That's sad. The better we *get* to know Jesus, the more we *want* to know Him. Why shouldn't it be that way in the ministry? Shouldn't we want people to know us better?

As ministers, we preach family unity and restoration because we know if the family is strong, the Church and the nation will be strong. Why then do we fail to realize the value of strong interpersonal relationships? We don't fear rebellion if moms and dads get along. Why would we fear rebellion if moms and dads get along with other moms and dads?

After reading this entire book, I believe you will be convinced, as I am, that the G-12 cell concept is what we need in the Church to prepare for the end-time revival. I invite you to take the plunge. It might not be easy, but it will be worth it!

How The G-12 Structure Works
Chapter 10

To fully understand and appreciate why the G-12 cell system works so well, we first must come to a knowledge of who we are in Christ. That knowledge begins with the basic understanding that we are three-part beings, made up of *spirit*, *soul*, and *body*.

I remember my science teacher at school, standing in front of a wonderful wall-sized chart and informing us that everything in the universe falls into one of three categories: plants, animals, or minerals. Everyone eliminated themselves from being a mineral after the teacher briefly explained what minerals are. After a somewhat more lengthy discussion, most were convinced they were not plants as well.

Drawing the class discussion to a conclusion, the teacher asked, "Who are minerals?" No one raised his or her hand.

"Good," she said. Then she asked, "Who are plants?" After a little hesitation, one little girl raised her hand. The teacher gently rebuked her. At last came the final question. "Who are animals?" We all excitedly raised our hands. But according to the Bible, we were all wrong!

You see, Paul said that in Christ, we move beyond living as brute beasts, chasing after the lusts of the flesh. Now we are being transformed into the image of God.

The teacher had just taught us that all humans are only brute beasts, "party animals." But that premise is completely against sound Bible doctrine (2 Peter 2:12; Jude 10). The truth is, the greatest of all miracles occurs when a human being leaves the animal kingdom and enters the Kingdom of God at the moment of salvation.

Being born again gives us faith for all the other changes we must endure as we are transformed into the image of Christ. We are spiritual beings, much more complicated than plants or animals. Far more than biology is required to figure us out.

In Second Corinthians 5:17, Paul said, *"Therefore if any man be in Christ, he is a new creature: old things are passed away; behold, all things are become new."* Paul was talking about more than having our sins forgiven. He was giving us insight into our new supernatural natures. When we are born again, our spirits receive the life or the Spirit of God, the very image of God that Adam and Eve lost in the Garden of Eden.

Paul gets into it a little deeper in Ephesians 3:17-19:

That Christ may dwell in your hearts by faith; that ye, being rooted and grounded in love,
May be able to comprehend with all saints what is the breadth, and length, and depth, and height;
And to know the love of Christ, which passeth knowledge, that ye might be filled with all the fulness of God.

It's hard to comprehend it, but Paul says we are four-dimensional creatures patterned after God Himself. Paul wrote this at a time when three dimensions were not even understood. The Greek word for the word "depth" is *bathos* and figuratively means *mystery*.[10] In Paul's day, what else would a person call "the fourth dimension"? Actually, the four dimensions are *height, width, breadth,* and *time.* Time, then, is the fourth dimension.

[10]*James Strong, Strong's Exhaustive Concordance of the Bible, "Greek Dictionary of the New Testament" (McLean, Virginia: MacDonald Publishing Co.), p. 18.*

The Bible is the only religious book in the world that acknowledges life in four dimensions. Nothing is impossible for those "new creatures," because they can tap into a multi-dimensional Heavenly Father!

We are four-dimensional creatures created in the image of a Spirit Being who has far more than four dimensions (Gen. 1:26). We possess a body, a soul, and a spirit (1 Thess. 5:23), and we exist in a single-plane time continuum. Although we are limited to four dimensions in our current physical state, we are still created in the image of a multi-dimensional God.

Consider a photograph, for example. It is a two-dimensional image of a four-dimensional object. So just like a photographic image of a multi-dimensional object, we were created in the *image* of God, but we do not have the same dimensions as He does. God has an unlimited dimensional existence, creating additional dimensions at will. This truth can help us understand miracles. You see, a miracle is simply a jump in dimensions from our ability into His ability.

The G-12 Multiplies And Never Divides

Now let's take this multi-dimensional understanding and apply it to the G-12 cell system. Traditional cell systems that divide at some point would be great if we operated only in a flesh realm, but we don't. If we are truly sons of God, we should be operating in the Spirit realm (Rom. 8:14).

Traditional cell systems resemble the Old Testament pattern as set forth by Jethro after seeing Moses trying to minister to the multitudes. Jethro advised Moses to give authority to capable men to rule — some over thousands, others over hundreds, some over fifties, and others over tens. Although these leaders were in covenant with the one and only true God, they were still spiritually dead. No one was born again until Jesus' generation, centuries later.

The traditional 5 x 5 cell system does a great job of organizing our souls into small corporate units, but it does a poor job of dealing with our *spirits*. This system's dividing nature works against our desire for eternal fellowship. Our spirits grieve whenever we are separated from loved ones.

Once we are in the Spirit, we must not return to the flesh (Gal. 3:3). As born-again, spiritual beings, we have unique needs. The G-12 cell structure is superior to any other system because it addresses the entire person: body, soul, and spirit. With the G-12 system, a cell is never *divided*; it is *multiplied*. Therefore, G-12 addresses the spiritual needs of the saint better than any other church-governing system. Little wonder that Jesus used a small group to evangelize the world!

Structure for a G-12 or 12 x12 Cell System

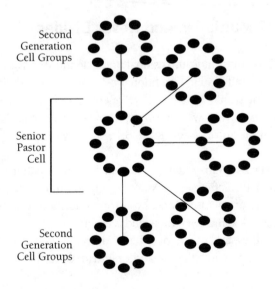

Second
Generation
Cell Groups

Senior
Pastor
Cell

Second
Generation
Cell Groups

FIGURE 2

Look at the difference, the G-12 is much simpler and easier to use! In the G-12 the Senior Pastor is right in the middle, not at the top, removed from what is going on. Almost all the paper work is eliminated because it is not needed. In this system, everyone can have the same position of 'middle' if they work as hard as the pastor. In the G-12 everyone is a disciple first, and then a cell pastor. The positions never change, thus eliminating all the politics.

The G-12 Proposition

G-12 stands for "Group of 12." It is sometimes referred to as the 12 x 12 cell structure and is comprised of a leader with 12 units. A unit may be a single individual; it may also be a married couple with or without children. The G-12 system is patterned after the New Testament example Jesus set forth while He ministered on earth.

The vision of the G-12 cell structure is simple. Twelve people or couples are united around a leader (or a married couple who co-lead the group). This leader pours his or her life into these disciples. Each disciple is asked to do the same by gathering 12 people around him or her to form a new cell group. The church grows by the thousands as each G-12 generation builds upon another.

Expectations From the 'Model of 12'

The vision of the G-12 cell structure is to cause the group of 12 to become solid pillars of prosperity. I am not referring to prosperity only in a financial sense, but prosperity in all aspects of life: prosperity in character and personal relationships; prosperity that overflows into the lives of others, multiplying the Kingdom of God. All these things are byproducts of the vision's success (Isaiah 60:21, 22; 65:21, 22).

Although the model of 12 is organized and intelligent, it takes time and commitment. Therefore, in order for the G-12 vision to be realized, it must be engaged with zeal.

This model generates strong friendships between its participants because the life of each member is seen as a real treasure. This brings lasting credibility into the relationships that are formed within the group of 12.

Consider the relationships that developed between Jesus and His 12 disciples as they passed the time together. This model that Jesus gave His people to follow generates a great sense of responsibility among the members of the cell group. Members learn that loving one another isn't burdensome, but rather a joy. Thus, the model of 12 attracts the anointing, giving people the confidence to attack their objectives with victory in their hearts.

The success of the G-12 vision depends on our persistence in executing the model and developing unity. But nothing can compete with the model of 12 when we are all rejoicing in the victory of multiplication. Our priority is to win souls — to consolidate them, to disciple them, and to send them forth for the glory of the Lamb. The anointing on multiplication is addictive, because it prepares us for that great and terrible day of the Lord when we will hear, "Well done, good and faithful servant" (Matt. 25:23).

The 20/80 Law

The principle of leadership that governs G-12 is the "20/80 law." Every pastor knows this principle. Simply stated, 20 percent of anything produces 80 percent of everything. For example, 20 percent of the people give 80 percent of the money, and 20 percent of the people do 80 percent of the work.

Conversely, 20 percent of the least productive people take up 80 percent of the church leadership's time.

Therefore, if you want to *grow* your church, work with the bottom 20 percent who take up 80 percent of your time. People will think you're a nice person, and then others will come. But if you want to *multiply* your church, work with the top 20 percent and then train them to do the same. By working with the 20 percent who produce 80 percent, you can greatly multiply your effectiveness in fulfilling the vision God has given you for the church.

Actually, working with the 80 percent results in merely *managing* the church, whereas working with the top 20 percent results in *leading* the church — and it is the pastor's job to lead.

Even the world of advertising understands the principle behind the 20/80 law. There is a rule in advertising that goes like this: It takes the same amount of effort to persuade 100 percent of the people of 10 percent of your message as it does to persuade 10 percent of the people of 100 percent of your message. The 100 percent with 10 percent of the message never get to the counter, but a person will get rich selling to the 10 percent who received 100 percent of the message.

It works the same way in church. You can deliver 10 percent of your vision from the pulpit, or you can deliver 100 percent of your vision to your 12 and then ask them to do the same. The result is a much larger percentage of the people who end up with 100 percent of the vision.

Too many church leaders expend enormous amounts of energy trying to do the impossible, which is to deliver 100 percent of the vision to 100 percent of the people. If they began operating according to the 20/80 law, giving a small group 100 percent of their energy and their vision, their efforts would be greatly multiplied.

The 20/80 law will save you a mountain of wasted time. If you want the offerings to increase, don't try to get the ones who are not giving to give. Rather, work on the top 20 percent of the givers to give more. If you need more work done around the church, don't waste your time trying to convince those who are not working to cooperate. Talk to the 20 percent who are already committed.

I heard it once said, "Go with the goers, not with the stoppers." In order to multiply, you have to subtract, cutting out the dead wood and putting the halfhearted aside. God's Word says that pruning the tree ultimately produces more fruit (John 15:2). Pruning isn't cruel or heartless; it is merciful, making room for those desiring salvation. The lukewarm and the rebellious block the road to salvation; they must be moved out of the way.

It took me a long time to learn that. I was very afraid of offending people. I let the bottom 80 percent take all my time. But my labor saw much more fruit after I started delegating the work of serving the 80 percent to the top 20 percent. That is exactly what Moses' father-in-law instructed him to do in Exodus 18.

If you do not understand the 20/80 law, it will be difficult to understand how the G-12 cell system works. When you adopt the G-12 vision, you select your disciples for your G-12 cell from the 20 percent who produce; then you train your disciples to do the same. Gradually, those in the 80-percent group will begin to see the light and will start to produce. When they do, they will also be invited to become a disciple in someone's G-12 cell.

The Two Types of Cells In the G-12 Cell System

If operated correctly, the G-12 has both Multiplication Cells and Edification Cells.

1) **Multiplication Cells** are heterogeneous groups sometimes referred to by traditional cell systems as "open" cells, "target" cells, or "evangelistic" cells. All are invited. The meetings are open to the public. They can be no smaller than three people — one leader and two members. They can be no larger than 25 people.

2) **Edification Cells** are homogenous groups, often referred to by traditional cell systems as "closed groups." By "homogeneous," I mean the whole is comprised of parts or components that are all of the same type. For instance, an Edification Cell might be a group of only women, only men, and so forth.

Only those selected by the leader may attend the Edification Cells. They are not open to the public. These cell groups can be no smaller than three people — one leader and two members. They can be no larger than 12 members or couples plus the leader.

What Are Multiplication Cells?

"Multiplication Cells" are meetings attended by born-again people who have invited nonbelievers. The primary function of the Multiplication Cell is evangelism. These meetings reach out with the Gospel to the entire community. They are an excellent place to invite friends, family, or people with similar interests. They are a multiplication strategy to build confidence in the believers as they reach out into the community and express their faith. Secondly, these types of meetings build the church numerically.

Every Multiplication Cell is composed of at least three people. In the beginning, no cell should exceed ten people. After the leader has gained more experience, these cells may eventually consist of up to 25 people.

OBJECTIVE OF THE MULTIPLICATION CELLS

The objective of the Multiplication Cell is to win souls, to reunite families, and to conquer cities by touching people from every race, creed, social level, and gender, whether married or unmarried, young or old. The goal is to grow and to multiply throughout the entire city, state, and nation and even across our borders (Matt. 28:19, 20). Evangelistic goals are realized through strategic prayer, Celebration Services, and the organized efforts of the Multiplication Cells. The consolidation process, cell vision, and ministry networks also support cell evangelism.

The leadership does all it can to stabilize and mainstream all the visitors in the local body. In order to be effective, the methodology must be adopted throughout the entire church. Nothing less than the congregation's 100-percent participation in the cells should be the goal.

MULTIPLICATION STRATEGY OF THE MULTIPLICATION CELLS

"Three-people prayer" is a fantastic strategy that should be used in *all cells* to help the multiplication process. This strategy involves everyone in the cell praying and fasting for three people for one month. After the 30 days of prayer and fasting, the cell members share the Gospel with those people for whom they have interceding. The results have been excellent, because it tears down spiritual strongholds and sets short-term goals that can be evaluated.

This procedure is an effective way for a believer to begin his cell group. After the new cell leader has gained three new cell members through the three-people prayer method, the process can start over with these new members. The result is rapid growth through intercession.

Cell vision is a strategy for attracting people with like interests from outside their circle of family and friends. Cell vision examples might be a group of professionals, a computer club, or a group centered around intercession, missions, sports, crafts, hospital visitation, or prison ministry. There are hundreds of ideas to choose from. The group develops around the cell vision, which helps the members to bond and makes it more likely that the group will stay together.

It is important to maintain proper priorities. The cell vision is simply "focused evangelism." Group activities lend themselves to a Christian lifestyle that promotes fellowship and evangelism. The cell vision concept can even include geographical groups based on zip codes or neighborhoods. Whatever the vision, it is only a means to the end — soul winning! The cell vision is a secondary factor for assisting outreach; it never promotes itself above the vision of the church.

Ministry Networks are homogenous groups made up of six groups or categories: men, women, married couples, male young adults, female young adults, adolescents, and children. Ministry Networks support evangelism by pulling people together with like interests — similar, in fact, to the cell vision strategy. In most cases, one of the Ministry Network categories, such as "Men" or "Women," is the "cell vision." In these cases, the vision of the group centers on ministry to one of the homogenous groups.

The seven Ministry Networks can average between two and four conferences a year and are attended by leaders of the aforementioned groups. The evangelistic aspect is that these meetings are open to the public. This exposes the leaders to those beyond their own extended group, and draws in new converts with interests in the above areas.

Consolidation has follow-up procedures that support multiplication by helping to retain the fruit of evangelism. (We'll talk more about the strategies of *cell vision, Ministry Networks*, and *consolidation* later.)

Celebration Services, traditionally called church services, are less threatening than the intimacy of cell meetings for some people. These special services often work to expose an unbeliever to the anointing of the Presence of God. The church needs to have a friendly and nonthreatening way of distinguishing visitors from members at Celebration Services so the cell leaders can identify them. At our church, we use nametags — black letters for members and red for visitors. Nametags also ease any fear or intimidation that visitors might feel because they can easily be called by name.

MULTIPLICATION CELL LEADERSHIP

Cell leaders always need the permission of their group leader to start a new Multiplication Cell. The minimum prerequisite for cell leadership is faithfulness to the vision of the church and the church leadership. Remember, every person must experience the entire process of the vision, from the Pre-Encounter to the Re-Encounter.

HOW TO START A MULTIPLICATION CELL

At first, a person's attraction to join a group might not be a spiritual one, but more like the attraction a man and woman experience when they meet for the first time. In other words, the initial attraction may be based on external appearance. However, a successful, long-term relationship must be based on the Spirit, not on the flesh.

People may begin attending a Multiplication Cell because they want to meet new people or because they need comfort after a divorce or some other tragedy. Whatever their original motivation, people continue to faithfully attend a cell group not only because it is fun and edifying, but also because it feeds their spirits. The cell group gives them an opportunity to operate in the things of God in a conducive and receptive environment.

When Jesus called Peter to be His disciple, He got Peter's attention by showing him the power of God to catch fish. What better way to catch a fisherman! Nathaniel was an intellectual, so Jesus persuaded him by appealing to his intellect.

You catch people by appealing to them on their level and by showing an interest in something they are already doing. That is one reason a Multiplication Cell is never a Bible study. Nonbelievers never go to Bible studies. They do, however, gather with friends for a barbecue, for instance.

Our church has had great success with backyard barbecues. Who doesn't like to come to one of those? Appealing to the stomach works. In the comfortable surroundings of someone's backyard, invisible walls start to come down and friendships begin to form. The next thing you know, you have the beginnings of a cell group!

Once Jesus got the attention of His disciples in the natural, He began to show them His vision. We call it the Great Commission. He used the gifts of the Spirit to attract them. Then He started pointing them to the vision. Since Jesus was sinless, He represents the only perfect Example of how to build a church. How did He do it? With small groups.

THE 'WHEN AND WHERE' OF MULTIPLICATION CELL MEETINGS

The cells meet every week in homes, offices, factories, schools, restaurants, or in any fixed location. They meet at any previously arranged time on any day during the week, as long as they do not hinder its members from attending the church's Celebration Services. They meet once a week anywhere from one to two hours. It is important that the church does not restrict the cells in their pursuit for souls by limiting cell meetings to particular days or times.

THE EMPHASIS OF THE MULTIPLICATION CELL MEETINGS

Multiplication Cells are not mature groups, so for the sake of the nonbelievers who are present, it is necessary to avoid unknown manifestations of spiritual gifts. Because of the participants' lack of maturity, they may not be able to correctly discern the prophecies, voices, visions, revelations, etc.

All emphasis in the Multiplication Cell is on evangelization. Spiritual growth comes through the edification and discipleship of the G-12 (or the Edification Cell, discussed later). The leader edifies the group through the Word of God. Those attending are encouraged to ask questions and participate in the discussion. The lesson is simply a platform for the group's edification and motivation, so a leader should be careful to stay away from Bible studies; they tend to alienate newcomers and stifle communication. Also, there should always be a time of praise and worship. (We'll talk more about cell procedures later.)

What Are Edification Cells?

Edification Cells, also called "G-12s," are homogenous groups in harmony with the Ministry Networks. Couples disciple couples; men disciple men; women disciple women; young male adults disciple young male adults; young female adults disciple young female adults; adolescents disciple adolescents; and children disciple children. (Children and adolescents are discipled with adult supervision.) Only people who are invited by the cell leader may attend the meetings; visitors are not welcome in this forum. The process of discipleship and edification occurs through these groups.

WHAT ARE G-12S?

The system is named after groups of 12, also called "G-12s." These groups are what sets the G-12 system apart from all other cell systems. G-12s are homogeneous groups, composed of 12 disciples or 12 couples who are ministered to by a leader (or two co-leaders if it is a couples' group). In order to be a member of a G-12, a person must be a leader of a Multiplication Cell or a G-12. Hierarchies are formed by these increasing generations of disciples.

The vision of the G-12 cell church is to make a leader out of every disciple. Each leader is at the center of his organization. All leaders have the potential for unlimited growth, no matter what generation of disciples they belong to. In the quest to produce leaders, everyone in the G-12 system except the senior pastor is first a disciple and then a discipler.

GOAL OF THE G-12

The purposes of the G-12 are many. Here are a few of its purposes:

• To greatly facilitate communication throughout the entire church.
• To allow every individual to be personally discipled.
• To ensure that the vision of the church is communicated in the same language.
• To ensure that the anointing flows unrestrictedly.

Among the many objectives of the G-12s are the development of spiritual gifts and the maturing of the saints. Spiritual manifestations and the anointing of the Holy Spirit are stimulated in the G-12 meetings, where the equipped leader can oversee and take responsibility.

THE TRANSITION FROM MULTIPLICATION CELLS TO G-12 CELLS

The success of the G-12 cell system is absolutely dependent on the effective transition from Multiplication Cells to G-12 cells. The mastery of this process cannot be overstated. The transition from Multiplication Cells to G-12 cells is absolutely key to the entire process. It is extremely important that all members of the G-12 understand this, especially the leaders.

A G-12 grows out of a Multiplication Cell. In the beginning, anyone and everyone is invited to attend the Multiplication Cell Meetings. People are asked to come forth for salvation, healing, and reconciliation.

A Multiplication Cell ministers to the needs of the new believers. It starts out as an open, evangelical cell meeting and moves slowly into consolidation. As the group grows, the leader doesn't prepare for a split, as would be true in the traditional cell system. Instead, he starts consolidating his group by selecting his disciples from among the members of his Multiplication Cell.

The G-12 never divides; it only multiplies. Although the group is open to visitors, the leader is careful to continually work toward the day when the group will be completely closed and consolidated into a G-12 unit. Thus, the Multiplication Cells form a kind of "farm team" from which to pick prospective G-12 cell members. (This concept is derived from the "farm teams" that major-league baseball teams maintain, from which they develop and observe young talent in a professional setting in order to select the best players for major-league competition.)

Jesus did the same thing. He didn't casually walk down the shores of the Sea of Galilee and pick the first 12 men He saw! He observed their work habits, watching them closely and discerning their hearts. After He had prayed and discerned the Father's will, Jesus commanded these 12 men to follow Him.

But we must also look at what Jesus *didn't* do. He didn't tell the group to divide after they reached a certain size. Jesus told them to multiply, to add to themselves, and that is exactly what happened in Acts 6:1-7, 9:31, and 12:24. Acts 6:7 states it well: *"And the word of God increased; and the number of the disciples MULTIPLIED in Jerusalem greatly...."*

It is extremely important that a person is observed in the Multiplication Cell before being selected as a disciple in the G-12. Therefore, the leader needs to observe the members in his Multiplication Cell, discerning those he believes are ready to follow him under all circumstances and be trained into leaders.

As the Multiplication Cell grows and the leader gains experience with the members, emotional bonds will begin to develop. As trust develops, it becomes very easy for the leader to decide whom he wants to work with. As relationships begin to develop in the Multiplication Cell, the leader selects people he would like to disciple. Not only would the leader prefer people whose character works well with his, but he is also looking for personalities that will balance and complement each other.

Selecting your ministry team is one of the biggest challenges of the G-12 system. Understand, however, that this process is not like lining up a bunch of little boys in front of a fence and picking out a team for a game, leaving those who are unselected feeling unworthy and rejected. Once again, Jesus is your Example. Brotherly love and fellowship are extremely critical here, moving you and the other members into your eternal destiny as brothers in Christ.

Your G-12 is a fraternal group, so when you invite someone to be a part of it, you are making a long-term commitment to that person. As your disciples grow spiritually, you can study their interactions in order to base future disciple selections on the knowledge gained from the accumulated wisdom of past selections.

Not only does the G-12 deal with our souls and bodies, but it also successfully deals with our spirits and our desire for eternal fellowship. We are made to commune forever in the Presence of our Father God. Therefore, we need to be more eternal-minded. Our family and friends here on earth will be our eternal friends in Heaven. In view of all these facts, careful selection of our G-12 group is an absolute key to its long-term success.

Once a Multiplication Cell leader has two committed disciples, he can start his G-12 cell with permission from his own cell leader. This means that during the transition period, the leader will conduct two meetings a week, one with his Multiplication Cell and the other with his G-12 cell group. This transition period lasts until he has filled up his group of 12 and turned his Multiplication Cell over to one of the disciples in his G-12.

The two meetings that the Multiplication/G-12 Cell leader is conducting, plus the meeting he is attending as a disciple, is a responsibility that inspires the Multiplication/G-12 Cell leader to move through this transition period prudently so he can return to only two meetings a week. More than anything else, this process is what sets the G-12 apart from other cell systems.

HOW A G-12 IS FORMED

A G-12 is created when at least two disciples come together under an approved G-12 leader. The G-12 vision requires attending two meetings a week — one as a disciple and one as a leader. Once someone is consolidated into a G-12, eternal bonds are formed. A decision to leave would be tough because, in a sense, it would be like a divorce. That is why once a G-12 is formed, it is so successful at building the church at large.

The minimum number of people that can form a G-12 is three — the leader and two disciples. The maximum number of people is 13 — the leader and his 12 disciples. The only exception is a couples' G-12 where the maximum number of members is 26 — the couple who serves as leaders plus 12 other couples.

INNER CELL DYNAMICS

Both scientists and psychologists tell us that although a single man can supervise thousands, he can only direct four or five. This is another important key to the success of G-12.

Your primary goal is to develop relationships with three or four families. In turn, you are fostering their relationship with others in the group. The dynamics are symmetrical. Each cell leader has three or four close friends, and each of them has three or four close friends — all of whom are the disciples of your G-12.

Let us look at Jesus' example. He had Peter, James, John, and sometimes Andrew in His inner circle. Michelangelo beautifully captured this concept in his painting of the Last Supper. After careful observation of that painting, we can see that Michelangelo grouped the 12 into four groups of three standing around Jesus. The head of each group is in Jesus' inner circle. The others follow behind these four in various degrees.

When Jesus went to raise the little girl from the dead, did He take all His disciples? No, He took only those closest to Him. That is the way it will be in any healthy G-12 group. A good cell leader will be careful to look for and develop these leading personalities.

Time can be another limiting factor. A lot of great people are out there, but we only have time to develop meaningful relationships with a few. Moses led more than three million people, but he had a close relationship with only his wife, Hur, Joshua, and Aaron. How did he move a nation? He had his inner circle of four and his outer circle of 70, according to Exodus 24:1-9. Do you see a pattern here?

Jesus had 70 in His outer circle as well. That is exactly how the G-12 cell structure works. The senior pastor moves his group, and his group members in turn move their groups.

Upon closer observation, we can see that the three or four leaders of the group of 12 lead the other eight or nine. These 12 then lead the three or four leaders in their own groups of 12. This process continues until, finally, the whole local body is led! It worked for Moses, and it worked for Jesus. Do we need more proof that the G-12 cell structure works?

When making your list of intimate partners, Jesus should always be first because He is the primary personality in your life. You also need to count your spouse and your children as the primary people in your life after Jesus. (The fact that many ministers forget this is probably the reason so many children born into the parsonage go astray. They resent the ministry because it stole their parents from them.)

After you have put Jesus and your family in their proper place in your life, this leaves you with two or three more open spaces. These spaces need to be filled with people who are really close to you. If you are single, as the apostle Paul was, you have extra room in your life for discipleship.

There are only four or five inner circle positions in your life, so carefully select who will fill those positions. But how do you know who to put in your inside circle? What happens to those who are not selected for this circle? How do you keep folks from being offended if they are not selected? Let me address these questions one at a time.

Offense is one of the major causes of stunted growth in the Body of Christ. Many have left churches and stayed away because they became offended. Jesus Himself said offenses would come (Luke 17:1). Even His disciples were offended at times.

How do you handle potential offense within your church? Let's look at how Jesus handled it.

When the mother of James and John asked Jesus to make her sons numbers one and two in God's Kingdom by placing them at His right and left hand, this request offended the other disciples. Jesus used great wisdom in His answer so as not to further offend the other disciples nor disparage the sincerity of the mother asking the question. He said that the best positions are reserved for those who serve the most (Matt. 20:27). According to Jesus' words, the Father will determine the intents of each heart and will properly reward those who served others for His sake on this earth with eternal honor and position in Heaven.

Therefore, when selecting your disciples, find out who is willing to serve more than the others. It can even become a kind of Holy Ghost competition in serving. Competition is not negative if it is based on serving and not receiving. Observing your members' level of serving will give you a good idea of who is in your group and where they fit in. Selection and promotion based on serving also eliminates complaints from those who might otherwise feel unjustly passed over in the selection process.

The message in the G-12 system is this: If you want to be promoted to the inner circle, serve. To desire advancement in the Kingdom of God is not wrong. Indeed, Jesus did not rebuke His disciples for desiring a promotion when they were arguing about who would be greatest. He simply told them how to do it — by serving.

Those in true Christian leadership do not hope to advance through politics. They know they are promoted to leadership by service. Any godly individual wishing to be promoted by God need only look for positions in which he or she might serve.

Jesus is God, yet even *He* came to serve, even unto death on the Cross. Jesus gave it all in serving. Why should we expect any less from ourselves?

I trust you can now see more clearly that which may have seemed complicated earlier. You will be happy to know that selecting disciples and then helping each one of them find his position in the group will all occur naturally. As cell leaders are faithful in service to you as pastor, doing all they can to serve your vision, God will send men to serve their vision as well. If the cell leaders are faithful to track down first-time visitors, follow up on absentees, and motivate and encourage those around them to do the same, their cells will grow.

You see, people congregate where the love of God is. A place of godly fellowship and communion will draw people. As the leadership demonstrates the love of God in their own lives, they will find that building a cell system is easy. The challenge is to develop God's character in people while loving them into the Kingdom of God.

WHY TWELVE?

Twelve is the number that speaks of a perfect total in God's economy. It represents perfection both in science and in knowledge. A day has 12 hours; a night has another 12. A year has 12 months. A clock has 12 numbers. (Would it work if a clock had 11 or 13?) Israel had 12 banners when it left Egypt (Num. 10:11-28). Jacob had 12 sons, from whom the 12 tribes of Israel came (Exod. 28:21).

Joshua separated 12 stones, on which he wrote the names of the 12 tribes (Joshua 4:1-10). There were 12 men who went to spy out the Promised Land (Num. 13:1-16). How many prophets were there in Israel in Moses' day? Six groups of 12. David had 12 chiefs of the tribes of Israel (1 Chron. 29:6). Solomon had 12 chiefs called princes (1 Kings 4:7). Jewish warriors were organized into platoons of 12 men. To set up a legal community in Israel, 12 men were needed (in other words, ten men plus the officiate and the rabbinical authority).

There were 12 baskets gathered in the miracle of the multiplication of the bread and the fish. For 12 years, the woman with the issue of blood suffered from hemorrhaging until she finally found Jesus. Jairus' daughter was 12 years old when Christ resurrected her.

How many gates does the New Jerusalem have? Twelve. How old was Jesus when He went up to Jerusalem to take His Bar Mitzvah? Twelve (Luke 2:42). How many disciples did Jesus have? Twelve (Luke 6:13). How many apostles were anointed? Twelve (Matt. 10:2-4; Acts 1:26; 6:2).

According to modern educators, 12 is the best number of students to form a class. Twelve is the number of perfect government. Twelve is the number of balance and functionality, and 12 is the number that speaks of harmony. The number 12 is also the number of qualitative administration. Billy Graham, Ralph Neighbor, Laurence Kong, and David Yonggi Cho approve of and encourage the model of 12, calling it the model for this millennium.

The vision for the model of 12 must be in the heart (Exod. 28:15-21). This model gives the priesthood back to us. It gives us an efficient team (Exod. 28:3). Besides all this, the true reason to collect local bodies of believers into groups of 12 is that Jesus did it. What greater and better reason could we have?

THE JUDAS SYNDROME

Let's address the issue of unfaithfulness in the church or the cell. I have spoken with several G-12 leaders who consider the twelfth man to be bad luck. I call it "the Judas syndrome." The Judas syndrome — sometimes referred to as "the Absalom spirit" — is an element of the cell that worries pastors the most. After all, they reason, if Jesus had one disciple go bad on Him, how can they expect to do better?

Several leaders have suggested establishing groups of 11 instead of 12 as a solution. I personally believe we need to keep the G-12 system unchanged but endeavor to learn what we can from what happened to Jesus' group of 12. For instance, not everyone the leader picks to be a disciple will work out. It will also not be the end of the world if, after the leader has done his best in the selection process, someone asks to be transferred to another G-12.

I have a rule I've followed successfully for years: *Confront* rebellion and *carry* weakness. Confrontation is not bad if it's the solution to a problem. Too many times by avoiding confrontation we end up fueling the problem. If and when rebellion comes, confront it, no matter where it is.

It is interesting to note that the 11 apostles cast lots to fill the position that opened after Judas sinned and took his own life. They knew that they needed to maintain a group of 12.

Many times I have suggested reserving this twelfth position for a special case. I call it "the mercy seat" — a special place for a unique person. For instance, a single mother, a widow, or a physically handicapped person could be given the twelfth position in a G-12. (I have purposely not mentioned race here, because the selection of disciples should always be based on character and personality and never on race.) That special someone should be a person who will challenge the group to operate in love as he or she receives from and gives back to the other members. It should be a person whom you might otherwise never have chosen. Perhaps that person just didn't seem to fit in, or maybe his or her potential for leadership or growth is not perceived to be on a par with the rest of the group.

It is important, however, that this person still fit the group's dynamics. For instance, if it is a men's group, a woman would be out of place. This person should be someone who can still fit within the vision, but who challenges the rest of the group to come out of their comfort zones. I believe that was one of Paul's greatest contributions to the other apostles. He challenged them — and more than once, he rebuked them!

The selection of this last spot needs to be put before God, not man. That being said, I think you will be wonderfully surprised at what the mercy position can and will do for the group as a whole. I consider the last spot to be potentially the most powerful one if we let God direct us through the Holy Spirit to place someone who might not naturally fit in, but in the Spirit, fits in perfectly.

COMPLETING THE G-12

In the G-12 cell system, each person is a disciple first and then a cell leader. Therefore, once a G-12 is complete, it becomes a ministerial management team. In other words, it shifts into an administrative role as it helps its disciples establish their own G-12s and then work their groups into consolidation. By the time all 12 members have completed their own G-12s, they will have grown together quite a bit, establishing long-lasting bonds with each other in the process.

Thus, the G-12 grows exponentially. It never breaks up or divides relationships. It grows, nourishes, and multiplies itself. Once a church is firmly established in the G-12 cell system, it will become an awesome force in the community!

G-12 Objectives

Every G-12 cell has the same objectives: first, to complete the group of 12; second, to develop "descending hierarchies" of cell groups:

1st generation	12 disciples
2nd generation	144 disciples
3rd generation	1,728 disciples
4th generation	20,736 disciples

(NOTE: Descending hierarchies refer to the *preceding* cell generations and not to lesser or weaker cells. Each cell has the same potential as any other.)

As the members of the G-12 pursue these two objectives, they will be greatly challenged to grow and mature in the Lord. The leader of the G-12 needs to establish this objective from the very inception of the group. Strategies may vary on how to reach these objectives, but the objectives never changes.

THE DESCENDING HIERARCHIES OF THE G-12

It's revival time! But in order to conquer new territories and bring the spoils of new lives into the Kingdom of God, we need to act by the leading of the Spirit of God. We must also communicate the G-12 vision in a simple manner. No matter where a person is in a G-12 hierarchy, he has exactly the same position in God as anyone else, with the same opportunities to show forth His mercies.

The two-part objective of the G-12 is achieved in four stages:

1. Conquest of the 12
2. Conquest of the 144
3. Conquest of the 1,728
4. Conquest of the 20,736

G-12 — The First Generation: This first generation of disciples is harvested from successful Multiplication Cells. A cell leader's first aim is to achieve an organization of 12 that forms a homogeneous group of men, women, couples, male young adults, female young adults, adolescents, or children. The 12 come together through prayer and fasting as they are brought before the Lord for His approval (Esther 4:16; Luke 6:12-16).

The G-12 can be started with three people — a leader and two disciples. The group is composed of those who are leaders of Multiplication Cells and/or G-12s. Every disciple must be a model. Conquest is gradual.

In First Corinthians 11:1, the apostle Paul says, *"Be ye followers of me, even as I also am of Christ."* In the same way, we must look after the disciples, teaching them all that Jesus taught, helping them receive all they need from the Lord.

G-144 — The Second Generation: The second stage of the G-12 objective is the conquest of the 144 G-12s. All the guidance given to the first generation must be passed on faithfully to this second generation. We must live and love the vision, respecting it and keeping it alive inside of us.

It takes fifteen people (or couples) to have a G-144. This includes a G-12 leader and 14 disciples who lead their own G-12 cell groups. (NOTE: Remember, it only takes two disciples and a leader to constitute a G-12.)

This second generation can actually occur in several ways. If your G-12 is composed of 12 disciples, all of whom are leading their own G-12s; and if at least two of your G-12 members have disciples leading their own G-12s, that would be 14 G-12s — enough to constitute a G-144.

Establishing a G-144 could also occur in other ways. For example, suppose a G-12 leader had only seven people in his group, and only three of those people were leading G-12s. However, if each of those three had three or four G-12 leaders under *their* authority, that would represent the minimum number of 14 G-12 leaders that is necessary to start a G-144.

These meetings may take place once or twice a month, depending on the leadership. A G-144 meeting supersedes a G-12 meeting, rather than adding a weekly meeting. For example, if a G-12 leader's meeting is on Tuesday night, his G-144 will also be held on that same night, and his regular G-12 members will be present to learn and assist.

The G-144 meetings are much like a church service, including praise and worship and one agenda — *growth*. The G-144 meetings are business meetings for G-12 leaders only. The speaker(s) — the person or couple who developed the group — uses the meeting to inspire and motivate multiplication, to plan strategies for growth, and to coordinate evangelism.

The first G-144 meeting of only 14 G-12 leaders represents an absolute minimum of 45 people. The meeting is very exciting for all involved, especially for the leaders who developed the group. It is a real milestone in anyone's life.

G-1728 — The Third Generation: This third generation in the G-12 cell system replaces the G-144 when that leader's group grows beyond 144 G-12s. (NOTE: Although the G-20,736 replaces the G-1728, which replaces the G-144, the leader's G-12 is never replaced. So at any given time the leader may have a G-12, plus one of the following: G-144, G-1728, or G-20,736.)

A leader of a G-1728 has his G-12 group full (first generation); each member of the leader's G-12 has his own G-12 full (second generation); and at least two disciples in the second generation have begun their own G-12 meetings (third generation). Simply stated, a leader qualifies to begin holding G-1728 meetings when his descending hierarchies are made up of at least 146 G-12 groups, the size of which constitutes a "congregation" that is far larger than 95 percent of the local churches around the world.

Can you see what is happening? The G-12 system inspires faith by calling a group with a leader and two followers a group of 12. It calls a group of 14 G-12 cell leaders a group of 144. It calls a group of 146 G-12 cell leaders a group of 1,728, and so forth. As soon as a leader steps up to a new level, the G-12 cell system calls him on to still a higher level.

The G-144 can be accomplished by the sheer determination of an aggressive leader. But when a cell leader begins a G-1728, it means he has ascended to new levels of leadership skill and influence in the lives of others. Achieving a G-1728 is the result of a collective conquest, realized by the entire team having the same vision. It signifies that the vision is well established in the hearts of the cell leaders. It is necessary, however, to pray without ceasing and to continue to transmit the vision so that, rather than diminishing, it becomes even more successful (Acts 2:42).

The G-1728 meetings are like the G-144 in every way, except that more leaders are involved. The G-144 and G-1728 meetings are a type of ongoing Leadership School, constantly building leadership skills and networking contacts.

G-20,736 — The Fourth Generation The fourth generation is the climax of the G-12 system. Landing at this stage means you are transmitting the vision internationally. You have passed through the principal vision levels and are reaping the fruits that few have enjoyed.

A leader qualifies to begin having G-20,738 meetings when his descending hierarchies are comprised of at least 1,730 G-12s, representing thousands of followers. In order to achieve this level of success, the vision must be big inside the leader. The size of the vision in him will determine the size of his success. He has to think big to be big (Isaiah 32:8).

Large is the plan of God. It is His desire that *all* be saved. That's a pretty big vision!

As a leader, the size of your vision will determine the size of the vision of your leadership. If your vision is small, your leaders will have small visions. If your vision is big, your leaders will have big visions!

We can think big because our God is a big God. *Our goal is global salvation!* We have been given the divine command to fulfill the Great Commission. That means we must conquer all that stands between us and that goal (Gen. 13:15).

G-12 Leadership

G-12 leaders receive permission from their group leaders to head up a cell. The minimum requirements for being a G-12 leader are as follows: 1) he must be successfully leading a Multiplication Cell, and 2) he must be at least attending Leadership School. Remember, every person must go through the entire process of the vision, from the Pre-Encounter to the Re-Encounter, which includes the Leadership School.

HOW A LEADER SELECTS HIS DISCIPLES

Before you begin your selection process, consider this: *Jesus selected His disciples; they did not pick Him*. He did not walk along the beach calling out to everyone, "Hey, who wants to learn how to perform miracles?" He carefully observed the labors of the men He selected as disciples. He knew them and called them by name to follow Him.

In the same way, the leader of the G-12 is the one who selects his disciples. That is a major key to the success of the G-12.

In contrast, the greatest shortcoming of the traditional cell structure is that the leader does *not* select his cell group participants. Instead, the members pick the *leader*. That is the reason why the traditional cell structure has so many cell group dropouts and burnout cases.

The Multiplication Cell gives the leader an opportunity to observe the members of his group. It also gives the leader experience with the people until he knows whom to choose. Working with someone is always a good way to get to know him or her. That's why men and women date or go through an engagement period before they commit to marriage.

Therefore, a leader should think of the Multiplication Cell as an "engagement period" and the Multiplication Cell activities as "dates." He should look for people who pursue him.

You see, after a man asks a woman to marry him, he hopefully doesn't have to beg her to be with him; the woman *wants* to be in his presence. The same applies with disciples. They participate in a cell group because they *want* to.

Read how Jesus talked to His disciples. Jesus told Peter that he was full of the devil. Jesus also told the disciples on several occasions that they were full of doubt. Jesus finally asked God how long He was going to have to be with this bunch of unbelievers!

Can you imagine saying such things to pew-warming church members? They would surely leave the church offended and try to take all their friends with them! But working with a disciple is another story. Jesus could talk directly to His disciples because they *wanted* to be with Him. It was their desire and choice to follow Him, even when it was difficult for them.

The cell leader chooses the ones who choose to follow him. This aspect of the G-12 cannot be overlooked. Assigning people to a leader or group simply by geographic division or for any other reason just doesn't work as well. Geographic divisions generally result in politics, which Jesus called sin, referring to it as the leaven of Herod (Mark 8:15). Politics puff up without adding substance and should be avoided.

The power of the G-12 comes about because a person or couple has a vision for a group and then selects people with that same vision. When people are divided according to geography, there is a big risk that they will end up feeling stuck in a particular cell. When that happens, motivation suffers.

Remember, we are not under the Law but have liberty in the Spirit. Therefore, cell group formation based on "have to" or "must" doesn't work in the long haul.

WHO CAN BE A MEMBER OF A G-12?

The selection of G-12 members must be done with much care and prayer. It isn't the disciple who chooses the discipler; it's the discipler who selects the disciple. The father chooses his sons, and the children love him. The groups of 12 aren't composed of friends or buddies, but rather of people with like convictions that are generated by prayer (1 Sam. 16:7). Jesus prayed all night long to choose His group of 12 disciples (Luke 6:12-16), so it is necessary for a leader to pray regarding the selection of every member of his team!

Actually, even the leader doesn't choose the 12; rather, he searches for God's heart so he can choose whom God has selected. To discover whom *God* has chosen is the leader's challenge.

Leaders must be careful who they put in their cells because they are making a long-term commitment to each disciple. God has the best 12 for every single group. Therefore, when a leader is in close communication with God, he will select the perfect combination of characters, personalities, gifts, and callings.

The leader should observe a prospective G-12 member's spiritual maturity before he or she is selected. This will avert potential chronic problems in the group. Remember, the 12 are only the first generation, and the objective of a G-12 is fraternal in nature. Therefore, the leader has the responsibility to build a team that never divides or splits, a team that has the ability to a generate a G-144 and, eventually, a G-1728 or even a G-20,736 with which entire cities can be conquered.

Ideally, the disciples or the "children in the faith" who form a G-12 have been personally led to the Lord and then consolidated by the leader of the group. They can also come from among the Multiplication Cells that make up his descending hierarchies. It is necessary that the persons forming the G-12 are teachable, submissive, and aggressively pursuing a holy lifestyle.

HOW LONG DOES IT TAKE TO FORM A G-12?

Although a Multiplication Cell can be set up in a week or even a day, it can take quite some time to form a G-12. Do not get in a hurry and make a mistake. It might take months to complete a G-12. The 12 will not necessarily come quickly, but they *will* come.

Be careful about being too conventional when selecting the 12. Remember, *"iron sharpeneth iron..."* (Prov. 27:17). It is important to select people who get along together but can still challenge each other in holiness and evangelism. Quality will produce quantity, so don't waste time with those who do not bear fruit.

The transition between leading a cell group and building a G-12 could take several months. The drawback during the transition time is that it is still necessary to conduct two meetings weekly, which is not desirable for most people. However, a leader can greatly reduce the time it takes for him to build a G-12 by preselecting several members of his Multiplication Cell before he starts his G-12. Thus, preselecting G-12 members from the Multiplication Cell can reduce the number of weeks he will have to lead two separate meetings.

If you are beginning a G-12, wait until your Multiplication Cell is successful enough to have six to eight solid disciples you would enjoy working with in your G-12. (Of course, in order to have six to eight strong people for your G-12, you may have 20 or 25 people in your Multiplication Cell.) Once you have achieved that goal, you can start your G-12 with two or three disciples. Don't shock your Multiplication Cell by removing all your strongest leaders at the same time. Slowly, over a period of several weeks, start bringing into your G-12 the people you have already selected from your Multiplication Cell.

It is best not to reveal the names of those you have selected from your Multiplication Cell. Don't tell them who they are until it is time to bring them into the G-12, because you might change your mind and possibly offend them if they thought they had been selected but in the end were not. By using this strategy, you can greatly reduce the amount of time it would normally take to build a G-12 Cell.

What Is the Emphasis Of the G-12 Meetings?

Again, a cell of any kind is not a Bible study. It is a study of people using the Bible. Bible studies develop listeners, not participants! Neither is a G-12 a bunch of folks trying to figure out what the Bible means. No, a G-12 helps people in their growth toward God and others because fellowship with God and with fellow believers is the goal.

The meeting resembles a corporate board more than a church group. It is a business meeting revolving around the growth of the members' descending hierarchies, with teaching and discussions about leadership skills and applications. Topics also include accountability, holiness, family, service, faithfulness, love, joy, peace, longsuffering, gentleness, goodness, faith, meekness, temperance, and humility, as well as the gifts of the Spirit (Gal. 5:20-25). These are all topics that promote character development and growth. Again, there should be a time of praise and worship in every cell meeting.

The When and Where of G-12 Meetings

The G-12s meet at any previously arranged time on any day of the week, as long as they do not prohibit or prevent its members from attending the church's Celebration Services. The Multiplication Cells usually meet in the same place each week to facilitate evangelism. However, because the G-12s are open only to members, the G-12 leader has more liberty to frequently change meeting locations. Rotating locations is encouraged so members might have the honor of hosting a meeting in their homes. It is also very healthy for the group to be familiar with the location of each member's home.

The G-12 meetings are held once a week and can last several hours. As mentioned before, it is important that the church does not restrict the G-12s by limiting meetings to particular days or times.

G-12s and Their Vision

In any given church, most of the congregation should have the same basic beliefs, but not necessarily the same interests. A group built around a common interest has more sticking power than a group that only meets together at the same place every week. This, more than any other single factor, is what makes the G-12 the cell group model of choice.

The church's overall vision is: *"Win — Consolidate — Disciple — Send."* However, the vision for the G-12 cells is smaller in scope and more specific.

I would like to add that the pastoral staff of the church in Bogotá attributes much of their success to strict adherence of the vision of their G-12 cells. For example, if the vision of the G-12 is male young adults, then only male young adults are in the group. If the vision is married couples with children, then only married couples with children can attend. I know this sounds a bit legalistic, but you can't argue with their success. It seems to be very important to have the vision of the groups well supervised by the G-12 cell leader.

A G-12 vision is any common interest that unites the group — similar, in fact, to the cell vision discussed under Multiplication Cells. Every G-12 must have a vision or focal point, something people can identify with. Traditional cells call them target groups.

For most G-12's, the vision will be participation in the Ministry Networks. For others, the vision will extend beyond the seven Ministry Networks into such areas as technical fields, sports, intercession, finances, publications, or anything that gives a focal point of interest to the group.

Every G-12 must have a vision or it will fail. A common interest or vision can mean just about anything that is not contrary to sound Bible doctrine and that does not in any way promote itself above the vision of the church. The key is to keep it simple and straightforward.

The leader's vision creates strong bonds and lasting relationships, and each disciple needs to be faithful to it. When a disciple starts his own G-12, he can choose his own vision while still remaining faithful to his leader's vision. You can see why it is very important for each leader to choose his own members or disciples.

The spiritual fulfillment that accompanies the G-12 is why it is so very successful. It is not a burden or an ordeal — it's fun! It's not suffering for Christ's sake — it's a joy! The G-12 forms a clan around a common interest just as in earlier times when families formed covenants. This type of cell structure recognizes the human spirit's need for fraternal, lifelong friendships.

The Time Factor

Let's address two weekly meetings, a primary criticism of the G-12. Although some are strong opponents of these twice-weekly meetings, I don't believe it to be an obstacle, and I will explain why.

Only those leading a Multiplication Cell or G-12 are required to attend the two weekly meetings. If a person isn't a leader, he only needs to attend one. Two meetings a week might strain some, but the overall advantages outweigh the disadvantages. My question has always been "What are your priorities?"

Before you throw out the G-12 system because it calls for two meetings a week, consider the following: A cell is like a church in many ways. As a church grows, a pastor takes on staff to help him. Likewise, as a cell grows, the cell leader needs help as well. He deserves the same reward as a successful pastor — a break from the trenches!

Forming a close-knit and loving group around him and his family is the reward for a cell leader's labor. From this position, he can then help his disciples develop their own groups of disciples. He becomes a kind of "father figure" in their lives, helping them work out their callings. Instead of burning out, the G-12 cell leader's flame will burn on for Jesus!

In summary, this is where some have missed it. They believe that the G-12 involves a greater commitment because it requires two meetings a week. But they have failed to realize that in time, the principal meeting stabilizes with mature Christians. Unlike babes in Christ, these mature Christians require less time and make less emergency calls because they have learned to handle things on their own. The reward for a job well done is a G-12 that is rooted and grounded in Christ, with each of the disciples working to develop his or her own G-12.

Although most believe the G-12 requires a higher level of commitment, it actually stays level theoretically, unlike traditional cells that continue to increase in commitment. In the long run, the G-12 cell structure keeps more people in the system.

NOTE: For tips on how to reduce the amount of time it takes to build a G-12, please refer to the prior section, "How Long Does It Take To Form a G-12?"

The Secret of Growth

An interesting thing happens when the cell starts working to help their disciples form new groups. By closing into a G-12, there is a significant paradigm shift. All of a sudden, the focus of the primary group changes. It goes from "our cell problems" to "their cell problems" — from "What can I get" to "What can I *give*"?

This element is almost completely missing in other cell structures and is another reason why I believe the G-12 is superior to other types of cells. It allows the consolidated group to concentrate on the needs of others instead of on itself. It is also constantly training new leaders because the principal or consolidated group is no longer receiving new people.

The G-12 allows a church to explode because it consolidates people and never divides them. It produces 12 more leaders every time it closes into a G-12. In just a few generations, a G-12 cell system will encompass thousands of people in groups of 12.

The reason the G-12 causes church growth to explode is that the groups are released to train leaders instead of constantly receiving new converts. Thus, every G-12 is potentially a massive growth center. Of course, no group is above soul-winning or helping new converts. All the G-12 does is keep the group members from wearing themselves out by constantly working with newcomers.

A major responsibility of the primary group is to help share the burden its disciples are bearing with their new converts. Every single member of the G-12 structure has the ability to become the center of an immense organization. It is only a question of serving.

Failsafe Burnout

The tremendous thing about the G-12 cell structure is that the more it grows, the farther away each cell is removed from crisis management. This crisis atmosphere that comes from dealing with new Christians is the source of most burnout cases, so there must be a balancing factor. As the organization grows, working people cannot continue to give more and more time to its success.

That is a major shortcoming of the traditional cell structure. The leadership is constantly facing new believers and with them, a fresh batch of problems. Is it any wonder that so many burn out?

On the other hand, the G-12 system has two meetings a week for those in leadership. The time spent counseling on the phone after services or cell meetings is less because the leadership becomes less involved in crisis management. Thus, in many ways, the two weekly meetings save rather than cost time. In other words, the G-12 utilizes scheduled time to work on counseling and other needs instead of taking unscheduled time away from the family. In short, the time commitment in the G-12 system actually stays about the same, whereas in other cell structures such as the 5 x 5, it grows with the organization.

The G-12 structure allows the leaders who have successfully completed their G-12 to work through their disciples. The beauty of the G-12 structure is that it preserves leadership by guarding them against burnout.

The G-12 system has a built-in reward system. It rewards successful leaders by allowing them the ability to stay active in the vision of the church with less direct input but with ever-increasing results. The greatest reward, however, is success. It is extremely satisfying for a leader to see himself being reproduced through his disciples, and eventually through his disciples' disciples.

Actually, the challenge many churches face when using the traditional cell system is the amount of time it takes to keep them going. That is why many churches end up paying cell leaders who have more than 25 cells. This results in a large payroll — something that is not associated with the G-12.

Also, churches involved in 5 x 5 cells for more than a few years have as many ex-cell leaders as active ones. Why? Because they are burned out. Burnout is so prevalent in the 5 x 5 or open-cell structure that many churches have discontinued the program — not because it didn't work, but because the church didn't grow fast enough to replace the leadership they lost.

In the Korean church that made the cell concept famous, almost all the cell leaders were women. Why? The men were too busy working. G-12 solves that problem by diversifying interests as the organization grows, thereby multiplying without having to invest more time.

For this reason, burnout is a much smaller problem in the G-12 system. The G-12 system basically governs itself. Supervision is built in by establishing a ministry team to oversee every cell. The burnout often associated with being in cell leadership is reduced because, once the open cell consolidates or closes into a G-12, most of the emergencies and all-night sessions cease. The attacks of the devil don't stop, but mature Christians know how to better handle them.

Once a group closes to new converts, maturity can begin. Instead of dealing with the problems new converts have, the group grows in friendship, helping to mentor one another toward maturity.

How To Make the Vision Successful

It is the anointing that breaks the yoke, not the system. When a congregation understands this truth, it saves them a lot of time and causes them to resist working in the flesh. Success comes at a price; without paying it, the reward is lost and the vision dies.

When we give up things for the sake of the Gospel, we are more than compensated by the joy that is set before us. Living a sacred and faultless life dedicated to God draws into our lives the peace of God that passes all understanding (Phil. 4:7).

No matter what the price, how can we know what the will of the Father is and not do it? Would He ever ask us to do something we could not accomplish (Phil. 4:13)? Would He ever place a burden on us that is too heavy to carry (Matt. 11:29, 30)? Absolutely not!

Therefore, we must cultivate zeal for the vision! We are called to fight against the forces of hell, stand up against the strong man of the city, conquer the devil's territory, and recover the spoils (Mark 3:27, 1 John 2:14). If we believe this model is God's best for our lives and we desire the fruit of success, we must violently press in (Matt. 11:12), refusing to shrink from the vision.

The vision of 12 is one of zeal that cannot be stained by insubordination. If the vision is not followed, growth stops. Once it is embraced, it cannot be distracted with fruitless efforts that don't have purpose. The Lord is calling us to urgently take in the harvest of the last days.

The G-12 vision is one that inspires creativity. However, this does not give leaders the right to make exceptions to the vision. The senior pastor leads the vision. Any change to it comes from him. Unauthorized diversions from the vision have the potential to bring terrible harm upon the entire edification process.

What Not To Do In a Multiplication Cell or G-12

Let me stress a few big "don'ts" in regard to cell meetings: Never discuss problems or difficulties in the weekly meetings. Do not gossip or complain about the church, the leadership, or any members. Do not second-guess decisions passed down from the senior pastor. Resolve any problems that arise individually and privately (Gal. 6:1, 2).

The Multiplication Cells and G-12 meetings should only include discussions and conversations about God's blessings. Never discuss any challenge to grow or multiply without a solution. Remember, in your tongue is the power of life and death (Prov. 18:20, 21). Therefore, see to it that every meeting closes with excitement and anticipation for the week to come.

Ministry Networks
Chapter 11

As good shepherds, it is our responsibility to watch over our flocks, as well as to watch out for wolves. We need to keep an eye on the lost world in which our sheep live because the enemy has many traps set to try to lead the sheep astray.

We are also very busy in our role as shepherds over God's flock. We have to make sure that our sheep eat from the good pasture the King of Kings has prepared and not from the things of the world. It is easy to see why Jesus said we cannot sleep (meaning we can't be slothful or lazy) but have to watch and pray (Mark 13:33-37).

The Ministries of G-12

It doesn't require any special knowledge or skill to supervise the average flock. A single shepherd can easily oversee 100 sheep. On the other hand, the G-12 system is so successful at producing sheep that it requires *more* than one shepherd. These undershepherds form a network to properly keep watch over a large flock. This network of undershepherds groups the sheep according to the similarities in their characteristics, making it much easier to stop trouble before it gets out of hand or to recognize a wolf before it has a chance to kill.

These "sheep groups" are called Ministry Networks and are formed by cells. The Ministry Networks are in some sense homogeneous. Everyone in the group is of the same gender, marital status, and/or similar age. The Primary Networks are as follows: Married Couples, Men, Women, Male Young Adults, Female Young Adults, Adolescents, and Children. There are also Supporting Networks that form secondary groupings; the meetings of these Supporting Networks have specific emphases.

Ministry Networks are organizations within the church with specific objectives that are proposed by the church. They facilitate excellent protection and preservation of the flock. Usually the head of each Ministry Network is a married couple, appointed by the senior pastor to coordinate and manage the network.

Ministry Networks follow the direction of the local church and serve as a support for implementing the vision. They serve the cells with an "auxiliary vision." In other words, if a cell doesn't have its own vision, it will automatically fall under one of the Ministry Networks. This auxiliary vision reaches every person in his own social environment within its homogeneous context.

Most cell visions are also one of the Ministry Networks because of the extensiveness of the networks.

THE PRINCIPAL NETWORKS

Under the proposal that defines the Ministry Networks, a network must be homogeneous. Again, this means that the whole is comprised of components of the same type. For instance, there might be groups of only women, only men, only physicians, only musicians, or only teachers. This homogeneity creates stronger interaction and communication among those joining the church.

Homogeneous Ministry Networks are set up to deal on a day-to-day basis with the core or central body of believers, meeting the need of each group and, therefore, the church. For example, the Married Couples' Network works exclusively with married people. Everything this network does relates to marriage or the family. Each Ministry Network is also responsible for counseling the members within its group.

The following list includes the Principal Networks, which must be implemented for successful ministry in your church:

- Married Couples' Network
- Men's Network
- Women's Network
- Male Young Adults' Network (youth)
- Female Young Adults' Network (youth)
- Adolescents' Network
- Children's Network

SUPPORTING NETWORKS

Supporting Groups need to be created because they are essential to the support of the Principal Networks. Unlike the Principal Networks, they are subject to the needs of the local body. The following list provides some ideas of the kind of supporting groups you might need in your church:

- Intercession
- Praise and Worship
- Inner Healing
- Special Events
- Bible Festivities
- International Relations
- Missions
- Administration/Technical/Computer
- Ministerial Relations
- Celebration Services

It is extremely important to note that the *heads of each Ministry Network represent the members of the senior pastor's G-12*. There may be exceptions to this, but Ministry Network heads should at least be in the Senior pastor's G-144.

This way all the undershepherds can coordinate their efforts with each other for the purpose of advancing the vision of the church in harmony with that of the senior pastor. That is why the seven Principal Ministry Networks must reflect the needs of the senior pastor and the vision the Lord has given him.

OBJECTIVES OF PRINCIPAL NETWORKS

1. The goals of the Married Couples' Network are as follows:

• Winning millions of married people for Jesus Christ.
• Marriage restoration.
• Solidifying and strengthening marriages.
• Marriage orientation; discussing such topics as finances, how to raise children, sexuality, etc.
• Treating each spouse's own character through individual disciple guidance.
• Promoting events, such as banquets, retreats, etc.
• Organizing its own Encounters, including both the preliminary and culminating phases of the Pre- and Post-Encounter.
• Preparing seminars and family clinics.
• Preventing separations and divorces through premarital clinics.

2. The goals of the Men's Network are as follows:

• Winning millions of men for Jesus Christ.
• Furthering adequate spiritual growth for the man of God.
• Establishing God's life in men's lives.
• Generating commitment so others may be won.
• Organizing its own Encounters, including both the preliminary and culminating phases of the Pre- and Post-Encounter.
• Solidifying the well-being of the family.
• Preparing outings for evangelization and consolidation, such as group fishing trips, outdoor barbecues, etc.
• Conducting seminars on manhood, assuming the role of the priest and king of the home, etc.

3. The goals of the Women's Network are as follows:

• Winning millions of women for Jesus.
• Furthering adequate spiritual growth for the woman of God.

• Establishing God's life in women's lives.
• Generating commitment so other women may be won.
• Organizing its own Encounters, including both the preliminary and culminating phases of the Pre- and Post-Encounter.
• Solidifying the well-being of the family.
• Preparing outings for evangelization and consolidation, such as tea parties, fairs, fashion shows, etc.
• Conducting seminars on womanhood, the center post of life in the home.

4. The goals of the Young Adults' Networks and the Adolescents' Network are as follows:

• To create a favorable atmosphere through cell meetings for winning young adults of every social class for the Lord.
• To recover rebellious young adults who are social outsiders.
• To assist the Young Adults meetings that foster compassion and identification in order to attract new believers with the goal of salvation.
• To inspire every young adult and adolescent to understand and obey God's call on their lives (discipleship).
• To make young people conscious of the world's dangers, such as prostitution, drugs, satanic music, and so forth, targeting young adults who are lost in the vices of today's society.
• To organize large evangelical events and concerts in order to bring together many young adults and adolescents.
• To impact the city through appropriate church services with an emphasis on evangelism for these age groups.

5. The goals of the Children's Network are as follows:

• To evangelize children in every way possible.
• To attract children whose parents already attend church.
• To promote evangelistic events, endorsing consolidation.
• To transmit the vision in appropriate language for children.
• To involve them in the G-12 model, respecting their limitations.

• To teach the principles of the Word so they might grow up as part of God's Kingdom.
• To teach righteousness and respect for authority (Prov. 22:6).

6. The goals of the Supporting Networks are as follows:

• To assist the Principal Networks within their specialties.
• To support further growth between networks.
• To win souls for Jesus and enlarge the support group.
• To train in the Supporting Network's specific area for the purpose of promoting unity and the group's vision.
• To disciple so that members might grow spiritually and better serve the various networks.

IMPLEMENTING MINISTRY NETWORKS

Ministry Networks need not be included in the initial phases of starting up the G-12 vision in your church. It is necessary, however, to be planning for the day when they *will* be implemented. It is difficult, if not impossible, to maintain a large congregation without these added dimensions. The flock must be broken down into homogenous groups for proper supervision.

Before implementing the Ministry Networks, the senior pastor will have to do the following:

1. Ask for God's guidance in appointing leaders who will run the Ministry Network vision. The leaders must be very successful in their G-12, and even in their G-144, before leading a Ministry Network. A Ministry Network leader must also be:

     a. A teacher
     b. A mature believer, full of the Holy Spirit
     c. Experienced in Christian leadership
     d. An excellent discipler

e. A pastor
f. Disciplined
g. Respected in the community
h. One who identifies with leadership

2. Wait for the right moment to implement the networks. Ecclesiastes 8:5 says a wise man discerns both timing *and* the correct procedure. Timing is very important.

From the very beginning, the vision of the cell groups and G-12s should be in line with the Principal Networks. That way when the Ministry Networks are installed, they will complement the vision and strengthen the groups rather than cause chaos or confusion.

On the other hand, if the Multiplication Cells and/or G-12s are formed without regard to the homogeneous Ministry Networks, the cells will need to be reorganized as time draws near to install the networks. This reorganization will displace many believers, causing loss of both time and disciples.

3. Make a special event out of the inauguration of each Ministry Network. Invite the entire church to share in this significant day. Introduce the Ministry Network director who is being installed, along with any other directors who were previously installed. At this time, make their functions clear to the congregation and confirm their areas of responsibility. They must be anointed in the presence of the entire congregation and given full authority to fulfill all they have been commissioned to do.

Announce the day and time of the Ministry Network's weekly or monthly meetings. (Generally, only those leading a Multiplication Cell or G-12 will attend Ministry Network meetings.) This is also an opportunity to announce the various special events for the following year.

4. Installation of a new Ministry Network will include publishing the meeting locations and times, including all particular characteristics of the network. For example:

• Network meetings have to be held every week, biweekly or monthly, depending on the Ministry Network and the need of the ministry. The meetings must be held on a specific day and attended only by the leadership of that particular group.

• These meetings will stress the proposal of the Network, prayer, and consolidation of those coming into the Network.

• Network leaders will receive the senior pastor's guidance regarding what must be done in their network.

• Mass media promotion of the networks is necessary so the city will know that the public is invited to attend special events.

5. Supervision and development of the networks are the responsibility of the senior pastor and the directors of the networks. It is necessary to point out that every network must be implemented step by step until the entire local church absorbs the vision. The congregation needs to see the need for any given network being installed.

It all has to do with timing. When the pastor waits until the congregation is pulling on the vision, their response will be to supply the ministries necessary to fulfill the need. Thus, with the introduction of each network, the church eagerly engages itself more in the G-12 vision.

Implementing The Vision
Chapter 12

In order for the G-12 model to be introduced into a local body of believers, there is a progression of implementation that must be followed. This process all starts with one person — the pastor.

One Man

The G-12 church vision must be initiated by the senior pastor. The Multiplication Cells and Groups of 12 will never develop if this program is delegated to another. The fountainhead must be the senior discipler himself — no one else. He must be the source of the vision so it can flow forth from him to the congregation.

The pastor needs to love the vision. He must believe that God is placing into his hands a church that will impact his city. Only then will that vision spill over into the lives of his 12. With this conviction, he will raise up the first cell group and eventually his 12 disciples to implement the vision with 100-percent success.

These 12 disciples of the senior pastor will constitute the "mother cell," from which all the other cell groups will eventually be generated until together they have become a great living organism. After adequate training, each of the senior pastor's 12 disciples will raise up 12 disciples of his own. This will form the G-144 of the senior pastor and create the second generation of disciples. Each of the 144 G-12 leaders will then generate another 12 disciples, thus growing to G-1728, the third generation. Finally, the 1,728 disciples will generate the G-20,736, the fourth generation in the G-12 descending hierarchies. In this way, the entire church will be directly involved.

Depending on the interest and zeal of those in the group, it is entirely possible in time to go from 12 disciples to as many as 20,736 (Matthew 13:23). Once the G-12 vision has begun, the results are tremendous!

One Family

We must also understand that the G-12 cell church vision is a family system. To capture a vision this size, the entire family must be involved and committed. Therefore, the senior pastor, his wife, and his children are the nucleus of thousands of groups of disciples.

It is important to have the cells start in a homogeneous fashion, because eventually the Ministry Networks will be introduced. It is also important that the senior pastor's wife raise up 12 female disciples so each of them in turn can raise up 12 disciples of her own. Once again, this process has the potential of eventually attaining, respectively, the G-144, the G-1728, and the G-20,736.

The senior pastor's wife becomes the pastor or director of the woman's network. Her disciples must have the same level of integrity as her husband's disciples. (NOTE: The wives of men who are in the senior pastor's G-12 are not necessarily selected for the wife's G-12 because they may not all be well prepared to form disciples and work with other women. If this is the case, these women must become part of the G-144 and receive training until they are found suited to become one of the principal 12. (This also applies to the men's G-12.)

The senior pastor must assist his wife, closely monitoring her 12 disciples along with his own. He must also familiarize his wife with the vision in order to ensure sound development of the women's network. The pastor's children will start their own G-12 cells as well according to their ages. (In South America, ten-year-old children are leading their own Multiplication Cells and G-12s.)

The senior pastor's family must be ready to take on the G-12 vision; it cannot be any other way. The pulpit ministers cannot be teaching one thing and the pastor's family teaching another; such a situation would engender rebellion and distrust. Besides, once the G-12 vision is operating correctly, it is too huge to allow room for other distractions. The vision is no less than the quest to fulfill the Great Commission. Therefore, it must encompass the pastor, his family, and the entire church.

The biblical order for life priorities that I have often heard preached is as follows: 1) God, 2) Family, 3) Ministry, 4) Vocation. That sounds great, but I cannot find that order in the Bible; therefore, I believe it is contrary to sound Bible doctrine. This message gives us wonderful excuses to stay home on Sunday mornings or during any other church service or event in order to "be with the family."

We must not let worldly humanism creep into our lives. The reason we have the Word of God is that, if left to ourselves, we would selfishly gravitate inward, taking care of our own needs and forgetting about a lost and dying world.

Look what happened to Old Testament Israel. Instead of taking the truth to the world, they turned the Gentiles' court of the temple into a market of thieves (Matt. 21:13; Luke 19:46). Jesus entered the temple, turned over their tables, and threw the rascals out! Don't you think that was strange behavior for a God of love? No! They had rejected God's call for their nation, which was *to bless and to be blessed* (Gen. 12:1-3).

Many of us are so focused on the "to be blessed" part that we forget our responsibility to be a blessing. We are carried away by concerns about the cares of this world, such as family, security, and getting more *stuff* (Mark 4:2-20). In the parable of the sower, Jesus plainly tells us that a person who doesn't bless others because of his own selfish personal desires allows himself to be robbed of life and of his reward. We must walk according to the Word of God, or the same will happen to us.

Jesus had more to say about this matter:

But seek ye first the kingdom of God, and his righteousness; and all these things shall be added unto you.
Matthew 6:33

If any man come to me, and hate not his father, and mother, and wife, and children, and brethren, and sisters, yea, and his own life also, he cannot be my disciple.
And whosoever doth not bear his cross, and come after me, cannot be my disciple.
Luke 14:26, 27

To "hate your family" means to love them less than the furtherance of establishing Jesus as Lord and Savior of your life. If you really love your family, you will put God first all the time. Then when the devil comes to your door, God will be standing guard, and you and your family will be safe.

If your family is standing guard when the devil comes, you are in big trouble. Your heart has only one throne. If Jesus is not sitting on that throne, there is only one reason: You are in idolatry. In such cases, He cannot protect you.

If we really love our families, there is only one order: *"Kingdom business first — then our business."* We need to understand that when we take care of God's business, He will take care of ours.

The best insurance for your family's well-being is to be in the perfect will of God. Do you really think the Lord would destroy your family by overworking you? God is perfectly balanced, and if you are obedient to Him, your life will be perfectly balanced as well. Serve God with all your heart, mind, body, and soul, and you and your entire household will be greatly blessed (Matt. 22:37; Mark 12:30).

One Group

Jesus established His own group of disciples before He preached to the multitudes. Luke 6:17 reveals the order Jesus always maintained:

And he came down with them, and stood in the plain, AND THE COMPANY OF HIS DISCIPLES, AND A GREAT MULTITUDE OF PEOPLE out of all Judaea and Jerusalem, and from the sea coast of Tyre and Sidon, which came to hear him, and to be healed of their diseases.

Too many times pastors get it backward. They go after the great multitude before they establish their disciples. The fruit speaks for itself.

Often the pastor feels abandoned by his people because they do not follow him. The truth is, the people are not following the leader because he has not applied a basic law of leadership: He is trying to lead his congregation before establishing a hierarchy of command. That's like a general trying to lead an army without having any officers. Such a situation would only produce mass confusion.

This is the reason the typical church has fewer than 120 people. Let's go back to the military analogy for a moment. In order for an army to be built, there must be an adequate chain of command. That is why the United States peacetime military is heavily populated with officers. If war erupts, it is much easier to add the troops than it is to suddenly train the needed officers.

However, most pastors try to build up the troops before they have trained any "officers." I'm not talking about a deacon board or a group of elders. I'm talking about a group of dedicated disciples loyal to the senior pastor and driven by the Word of God — proven fruitful men with successful cell groups and G-12s, as well as proven fruitful women in the cell group of the pastor's wife.

The senior pastor's G-12 represents a "roundtable" of future generals commanding a vast army of God. No man should be in the senior pastor's G-12 who does not have the ability to become a general for the Lord.

Think about the pastor's selection of his G-12 the way you think of selecting a lifetime mate. When you decide you want to be married, you don't just pick the first person you meet. You make a decision based on love and on accumulated evidence that you are compatible with a particular person. You try to choose someone with whom you have something in common. This is the purpose of dating — to experience each other's likes and dislikes before making a lifelong commitment.

It works the same way in the G-12 vision. In a sense, the Multiplication Cell is the so-called "dating experience" that allows you to observe and to test the loyalty of certain disciples. Once you are certain a long-term relationship with these disciples would work out, you can arrange the "marriage" by asking those loyal to the vision to become disciples in your G-12.

The senior pastor cannot entrust the positions in his G-12 to the unstable, such as a man who is living with a woman out of wedlock. The pastor's goal should be to select godly men with compatible personalities who can form a holy team. This team must be founded on the understanding that the head — the senior pastor — presides at all times. The team members' role is to administrate his vision, making sure it is transmitted and conformed to throughout the entire church.

The success of the vision is the outcome the pastor experiences when he does well in selecting his 12 disciples. In the beginning, some in the congregation may attempt to discredit members of the pastor's G-12, referring to them as "the privileged ones," "the pastor's favorites," and so on. But God will give grace. After witnessing the tremendous anointing on the senior pastor's G-12 disciples and their honoring of their leader, the congregation will honor them with respect as well.

(NOTE: Not all the men or women who start off in the Multiplication Cell of the pastor or his wife will become members of their G-12s; however, they will all be in the senior pastor's G-144.)

The selection of your 12 must be preceded by much prayer. Once again consider Jesus' example. He was very disciplined at praying. He prayed all night long to choose His 12 disciples (Luke 6:12-16). In the same way, it is necessary that you pray by name for each of those the Lord gives you! Then wait until a person has produced fruit before inviting him to become a disciple.

Once you start selecting your disciples, you must point them toward Jesus, just as Jesus pointed His disciples to the Father (John 17:6). Never attempt to draw attention to yourself. *Your glory is not what men seek.*

Leadership starts to cost something when you find out who is with you and who is not. Jesus said in Matthew 10:39, *"He that findeth his life shall lose it: and he that loseth his life for my sake shall find it."* If people are not willing to lose their lives for the cause of the Gospel, they will never find true fulfillment. They must have a cause in their lives that they would die for.

Matthew 6:24 (AMP) tells us that there are two great causes in life:

No one can serve two masters; for either he will hate the one and love the other, or he will stand by and be devoted to the one and despise and be against the other. You cannot serve God and mammon (deceitful riches, money, possessions or whatever is trusted in).

Christ is the only cause big enough to completely fulfill us. The counterfeit cause in life is the love of money, which is more powerful at destroying men's lives than the devil himself.

Notice Jesus didn't say that the two greatest forces were God and the devil, but God and money! Think about it — what happens after you get money? Did joy come from getting the money or from spending it?

Suppose you go shopping, hoping that the purchase of a new car or a new dress will make you happy. But after the dress is hanging in your closet or the new car is parked in your garage, then what? Where will you find joy?

If we are not careful, we will go from toy to toy in an effort to find satisfaction. But true satisfaction never comes from buying bigger toys. It only comes from a personal relationship with Christ Jesus.

Yes, you can make big money and have nice things, but don't allow those things to have you. This is the test: Do you own anything you wouldn't give away if God asked you to?

People will often "talk a good talk" in order to hang around with the pastor and his wife. But when it's time to pay the price of commitment, many end up dropping out.

One reason the early Church grew so fast is that there was a price to pay. Yet pastors today often make a big mistake by trying to make the Christian walk as easy as possible so everyone can come to church and be fed the Word.

I fall into that trap all the time. Of course, we push babies in a stroller to get them to church. But we are not talking about spiritual babies here — we are talking about making *disciples*.

When an offense comes trying to split the church, the biggest "tongue-waggers" are always those uncommitted people who are just going along for the ride — the opportunists who are looking for something or someone other than Jesus. These folks need to be called out and eliminated.

The anointing comes with a price. You know you have a real disciple when his commitment to the group has cost him something, yet he has paid the price without murmuring or disputing. For instance, when I went to my first cell meeting in Southern California, I walked two hours to get there. In my eyes, it was a small price to pay for the privilege of being part of that group, and I became one of its most faithful members.

Part of discipling is making demands. When I say, "make demands," I'm talking about asking someone to take on certain responsibilities, such as taking care of the group members' children during that week's meeting, visiting a group member, or even coming early to a meeting to help set up. The old excuse, "I don't have time" doesn't fly after a disciple has established the fact that he would die for the Gospel. If he is willing to give his life, giving his time is but a small thing.

It all starts with a disciple's decision to give his life to God. When he becomes a willing servant, his time is given to God. Discipleship is learning to die to self so Christ might be glorified in one's life. The cell group puts this principle into operation by supplying a support team for the senior pastor, knowing that what they sow into his life and ministry they will reap in their own groups.

As your Multiplication Cell starts to grow, you will begin selecting your G-12 disciples. At the same time, you will be rooting out those who don't really want to work with you by transferring them to other cell groups. This process is a bit delicate, but it is vital to the success of the G-12 cell church.

It is crucial to be sensitive to those being moved into other groups, both in the same generation and in the next one so they don't end up feeling unwanted. Generally speaking, 95 percent of those transferred do not feel rejected because they realize they didn't fit the cell vision. Even so, those being moved to another cell must not feel like they're being dumped off. You must believe God that they will match successfully with one of your disciples or with another cell leader; then you must help them make the transition to that cell.

Consequently, by the time you have eight or nine disciples in your cell, many of your disciples may already have people in their cells. You don't need to wait until you have completely consolidated your cell for your disciples to start their own cell groups.

Before a cell group consolidates or moves into a G-12, it has only three kinds of people: disciples, developing disciples, or those waiting to be transferred. The people waiting to be transferred are actually waiting to meet up with a disciple who is starting a new group and whose vision is one they can embrace.

There is a place for everyone. Our challenge is to find it. If someone gets upset or offended about not being selected by a certain leader, they are free to go to any Multiplication Cell they choose. People who are asked to transfer to another group can use this as an opportunity for a character check, maturing wonderfully in the process.

In my church, I have discovered that if several people are in need of transferring to another cell, there is always a disciple with a vision who is ready to draw those people into his cell. Allowing leaders to select the people for their G-12s results in extremely strong bonds being formed.

The concept of people working together on a vision that they themselves have developed is called "ownership" in modern management. Ownership feeds creativity and enthusiasm. You never hear complaints such as "Those people you sent me just don't work" or "No one is getting the vision." The leaders selected their people, and it is their vision. If it isn't working, guess what? It isn't someone else's fault — it's theirs.

There are no excuses for a cell's lack of progression toward the fulfillment of its vision. No one is worthy of leadership if he is not willing to put down his own desires for the desires of our Heavenly Father.

I realize that, as you read this, you might find the G-12 system a little overbearing. But remember, it is a church-governing system that produces mega-churches! If you want the most successful church in your city, there needs to be great zeal hooked up to an effective method.

SENIOR PASTOR'S CELL ORGANIZATION

The Senior Pastor's G-12 must be an exemplary model of a G-12 cell because it is also the mother cell from which all others cells are birthed. I sometimes refer to it has the crown of the vision because of its central and commanding position.

The mother G-12 uses the inner circle of four disciples to supervise the vision. This is called "The Vision Supervisory Level" and includes four positions: Evangelism Pastor, Consolidation Pastor, Discipleship Pastor, and Celebration Pastor. These four generals are closest to the pastor and guard the integrity of the entire vision. Although all G-12 leaders and Multiplication Cell leaders are responsible for each part of the vision, these four positions empower the vision by enforcing it throughout the church and by coordinating the efforts of all the cells.

Cell leaders have a tendency to drift away from the vision or camp in an area they are most comfortable. The leaders in the Vision Supervisory Level maintain the vision's forward motion by helping the cell leaders keep focus and balance.

As mentioned earlier, the Ministry Network leaders should be in the senior pastor's G-12. The "Ministry Network Level" forms a second tier of authority in the senior pastor's G-12. Those who fill these positions are responsible for their particular homogeneous networks.

It is very important to understand that the senior pastor's Ministry Network leaders who are not heads of Principal Ministry Networks may lead any type of homogeneous cell group that conforms to the vision of the Principal Ministry Networks. For example, the Supporting Network "Praise and Worship" will fall into one of the seven Principal Networks: Married Couples, Men, Women, Male Young Adults, Female Young Adults, Adolescents, or Children. That means that even though the Praise and Worship Network is separate in purpose and vision from the Principal Ministry Networks, its vision is still encompassed in the framework of one of these principal groups.

The senior pastor's wife forms the head of the Women's Ministry Network. She has her own G-12, which resembles her husband's G-12 with the exception of the Vision Supervision Level. She will have her own inner circle made up of those closest to her. It differs because of the special needs and talents that the women have. In the wife's group, there can be women who are heads of Supporting Ministry Networks.

It is highly recommended that the senior pastor and his wife have different G-12s because separate-gender cell groups greatly facilitate the multiplication process for several reasons. The primary reason is that men and women do not act the same in each other's company, whether they are single or married. For instance, most men are too embarrassed to talk about sexual sins or other perversions and vices in front of the opposite sex. Women also tend to be much more inhibited in a mixed group. Therefore, having adults and youth meet in separate-gender groups stimulates fellowship and confidence.

VISION SUPERVISION

As mentioned earlier, few can have meaningful personal relationships with a dozen people; not even Jesus could do it while He was here in the flesh. So instead of attempting to do the impossible, the senior pastor needs to stay within the realm of the possible and keep his challenges realistic. Since he needs assistance to keep the vision moving, who can better provide that assistance than his four closest disciples?

The following are the responsibilities of the four positions of Vision Supervision:

1. Evangelism Pastor

• Supervises evangelism in the cells.
• Plans evangelistic events.
• Coordinates evangelistic events between cells.
• Motivates church members to participate in personal evangelism.
• Sends out cell leaders to start new works.

2. Consolidation Pastor

• Supervises consolidation in the cells.
• Phone follow-up.
• Personal visitation.
• Trains leaders to carry out the Pre-Encounter, Encounter, and Post-Encounter.
• Coordinates the consolidation process between cells.
• Sends out cell leaders to start new works

3. Discipleship Pastor

• Supervises discipleship in the cells.
• Trains teachers for the Leadership School.
• Stimulates cell growth and participation.
• Trains leaders to carry out the Re-Encounter.
• Coordinates discipleship between cells.
• Sends out cell leaders to start new works.

4. Celebration Pastor

• Supervises all church activities.
• Coordinates all church activities between the cell groups.
• Supervises church maintenance, security, and operations (e.g., bookstore, tape sales, coffee shop, etc.).
• Relieves the pastor of concerns about any aspect of practical operations that involve the church building or properties.

CELL REPORTS

All cell leaders should keep a binder of some type in which they organize the reports coming in from their cell members who are leading Multiplication Cells or G-12s. The binder should have a section for each cell leader's cell meeting reports; a pocket for blank report forms; and a page listing all the members of the group for the purpose of taking attendance. The binder should also have a history of the lessons used by the group and any other necessary history of the meetings or group members.

Although the simplicity of the G-12 system eliminates most paperwork, it is still important to keep a record of every meeting. At the beginning of every meeting, a report form should be signed by each person attending. An assigned group member can fill in any other necessary information. The cell leader then gives the cell meeting report to his cell leader at the next meeting. That leader in turn gives his cell meeting report to his leader. In this manner, the reports make it all the way to the senior pastor's group.

As each cell leader passes his cell meeting report on to his leader, he should attach copies of all other cell meeting reports that his leaders have turned in to him. For example, if a G-12 leader has three members with Multiplication Cells, he will receive three cell meeting reports a week. After making photocopies of these three weekly reports, the cell leader files the original copies in his binder. Attaching the photocopies to his own cell meeting report, he then gives the report to his leader.

Leaders should also keep a copy of their own cell meeting report for their records. This is a very simple and efficient process.

ADMINISTRATION

In Figures 3 and 4, you will notice that "Administration" is positioned right below the senior pastor and his wife. This is the position of the church administrator. In my particular case, the church administrator is not in my G-12; she is in my wife's G-12.

Whatever the church project, there is almost always money involved. That means there has to be accountability. Therefore, all church operations must pass through the administrator's office so that at all times, the whereabouts of church funds are known.

One Church

Who will participate in the G-12 vision? Men and women who love Jesus; who have committed themselves to God; who are well known by the senior pastor and his wife; who can be trusted; who govern their own house; and who are experienced in prayer.

The ministry must be completely committed to the vision. This will require the senior pastor's total commitment and that of every member, from the oldest deacon to the most recent convert. All must participate in a cell. Under no circumstances can anyone remain out of this new movement of church government. The entire church community must be committed to the vision (Isa. 41:6).

As we have seen, the cell-oriented church is a ministry that has its members directly involved in saving souls for God's Kingdom through cells and the model of 12. Starting with the formation of the first G-12, each member will be eager and motivated to complete his 12, to grow on toward his 144, and so on. At this point, everyone in the church will be engaged in direct evangelism — bringing in visitors, consolidating them, and turning them into disciples (Matt. 28:19, 20). In external evangelism, they will save souls in cells that assemble in homes, schools, factories, and so forth, raising up disciples and promoting the growth of other cells. Remember, the cells are live organisms; they will experience as much growth as we allow them to in our churches.

The Multiplication Cells and the groups of 12 must be spoken about from the pulpit. The vision must stay in front of the people all the time.

The cell-oriented church will develop programs and goals. It will always endorse its growth until it impacts both its city and its nation. Therefore, a cell-oriented church will always see its membership multiply in marvelous ways. God loves this project. It is the direction given by Jesus for His Church in these last days (Matt. 28:18-20).

We must expect that obstacles may arise as we pursue the G-12 vision. Satan will try to say that it is a "quantity without quality" strategy for church growth. Let's not trouble ourselves with such reasoning. The groups of 12 will take care of the discipleship of every individual. The goal must be to conquer the city. God is counting on the entire congregation to do their share and to believe in what they are doing under His leadership. Ultimately, He will provide the growth (1 Cor. 3:7-9).

These cell groups, or clans, form a rock-solid foundation on which the church grows. It works — just look at the Bogotá congregation! Their church is growing by the thousands every month! Within a few years, they will be the largest church in the world!

Why not get your church started in the G-12 system now? Why not be the largest church in your state? Why wait? It can work for you!

Prayer:
The Key to Revival And Multiplication

Many wonderful things will happen in your ministry if you carefully follow these steps. Give it some time — every phase must be implemented at the right moment (Eccl. 8:5,6). Before implementing the model of 12 — or anything else for that matter — a time of prayer is necessary. Prayer is essential for the church's growth and revival.

1. To build the church by prayer, conduct prayer meetings every morning (1 Thess. 5:17).

2. Involve the entire church in prayer — *in the church building.* Set specific goals so they will pray for their families, for finances, for personal goals, for revival, and for the nation.

3. Announce in the church that problems will be solved when we learn how to pray. That way people will start realizing they can do nothing better than to dedicate the first hours of the day to prayer.

4. Delegate the prayer hour to skilled people of prayer (cell leaders) so they will assume the vision of daily prayer early in the morning at the church. The church must comprehend that it is necessary to pray.

5. Don't be concerned about the number of people who attend prayer meetings. In time, people will show up, regardless of time, temperature, or transportation difficulties.

6. Ask a musician (or install a CD player) to fill the first moments of prayer with soft praise and worship music, during which people pray personally. After that, the minister opens a time of general prayer, which focuses on specific needs.

7. Make sure prayer starts and ends on time so it will generate confidence in those participating. If prayer goes over the allotted time again and again, it may cause people to drop out.

8. Persevere in prayer. This will set a solid basis for growth (Col. 4:2). Without prayer, we won't get very far in pursuit of our objectives (John 15:5).

The persistence of the dreamer is what makes a dream come true, so we must never lose sight of our dreams. We must pursue our dream and announce it in the Kingdom of the Spirit. We must keep nurturing it so we can *"...be like a tree planted by the rivers of water, that bringeth forth his fruit in his season; his leaf also shall not wither; and whatsoever he doeth shall prosper"* (Ps. 1:3). The prosperity of our dream can invade the nations!

Where To Start

The Lord admonishes us not to despise small beginnings (Zech. 4:10). Whether you pastor 5,000 or 5, the process is exactly the same. Assemble your 12 just like Jesus did. Pour your life into them, holding nothing back. When your disciples are ready, release them to do the same thing while maintaining their relationship with you. Isn't this what Jesus did? He sent them out, and they returned full of thanksgiving and praise for all the Lord had done through them!

Pastors of larger churches — both those that have been using a cell system and those who have not — will have a group of successful cell leaders or supervisors with whom they can work right away. In the case of smaller or newer churches, the pastor will need to be more careful about whom he pulls into his group.

Remember, all G-12s start out as an open cell, so don't make hasty decisions based on perceived needs. Wait on God's assistance in selecting the people for your cell group. If you wait and watch a person or a couple's performance and anointing for an extra few weeks or months before making a final decision, your patience could save you untold problems and challenges down the road. Every person has a place, but it might not be in your group.

The G-12 system will slowly begin to take over the church. Any pulpit announcements or coaching should acknowledge what is happening. The pulpit should be the place for edification and exhortation, *not* for condemnation of anyone who isn't yet participating.

It is very important to understand that the implementation of the G-12 model will take time. In some cases, it will take longer than you think. The best-case scenario in which to implement this cell system is a young church. In a new setting, the cells will take off quickly.

On the other hand, it can take years for the new system to be accepted in an established, traditional church. The "old guard" will usually fight it all the way. But just stay with the vision and don't get discouraged. In the end, the cells will bless the church in many ways. For instance, the congregation will have a leadership team that both understands the challenges of the ministry and shares a high level of mutual respect among team members.

That's why it's important for the congregation to understand that, under the G-12 system, all the veteran believers will not be cast aside in order to bring in the new ones. The veteran believers will be engaged in helping to fulfill the vision of the church. They will come to understand that they need to bear fruit themselves by multiplying and starting their own G-12s in the future.

How To Build Your Organization

We suggest that you visit a well-operated cell church to witness how miraculously the G-12 system works. There is nothing better than to go to Bogotá, Colombia, and see for yourself what God has done in that mega-church with more than 30,000 cells. Or you could go to Manaus, Brazil, to observe what the Captain of the Host has done among His people there. During that visit, you will be able to take a closer look at the G-12 vision, participate in an Encounter, and receive an anointing for multiplication.

I suggest the following procedure:

1. Pray and fast for your 12 disciples. As mentioned before, Jesus prayed all night long before He invited His 12 to join Him: *"And it came to pass in those days, that he went out into a mountain to pray, and continued all night in prayer to God. And when it was day, he called unto him his disciples: and of them he chose twelve, whom also he named apostles"* (Luke 6:12,13). The 12 disciples were appointed as Jesus' "apostles" or "missionaries." God will pick out courageous believers to walk by your side.

2. Hold a meeting to inform future disciples about your ministerial intentions. Explain to them what role they will play and how they will implement the vision in their cells during this phase. Also, tell them what God expects from each of them.

3. Take the 12 on a spiritual outing in order to explain the vision in greater detail. Spend time with them; listen to their dreams; and talk about your own ministerial dreams. Tell them

how and in what area of ministry each one of them might be useful. Pray together and make plans to achieve lofty goals. Plan to visit a well-organized cell church together as soon as possible. It will be good for all your disciples to see miraculous growth as a result of cells. In doing so, they will be motivated, and their enthusiasm will spread to others.

4. Stimulate your 12 disciples to pray for *their* 12. Through prayer and fasting, God will show them who their 12 will be and what He wants them to do. These disciples will form the second generation of your G-144.

5. If possible, when you visit the successful cell church together, attend an Encounter with all the candidates. Participating in one of the cell church's Encounters will help train you and your team for your future ministry together. During the Encounter, your disciples will go through a sanctification process that will greatly enable them as ministers of the Word of God.

6. Gather your group together regularly to pass on the vision and your dreams. Find out how every disciple is raising up his own disciples. Make all of them feel as though you are their spiritual father and you're looking after your family.

7. Get together with every disciple individually so you can become well acquainted with each of them. Know their dreams, problems, personal difficulties, etc. Guide them toward discipleship, giving them excellent spiritual care (Matt. 5:1,2). Cry with them; shepherd them (John 21:15-19). Don't get frightened because of their problems and difficulties. Show them your understanding. Inspire confidence, and share what you expect from each one in this new phase.

8. Set goals with your disciples in the managing or supervising of their own groups of disciples and the creation of their own Multiplication Cells.

9. Work with your disciples first to establish goals; then motivate them and control the fulfillment of those goals individually. Reward them collectively before the congregation for achieved goals.

10. Make sure your church speaks the same language and is "on the same page." Instruct your disciples to repeat all that is ministered in the mother cell (2 Tim. 2:1,2).

11. Schedule with the group both the fraternization meetings and dates for leisure trips. Remember, your group is a family unit and needs to have times of communion and fellowship. Sometimes the meetings can become so administrative that it is easy to forget about communion (Acts 2:42).

12. Establish the Leadership School in your church (2 Tim. 2:15). Pray for a schoolmaster to take charge of the Leadership School — someone who has embraced the vision. Initially, keep the vision of the Leadership School in front of the entire church so everyone can walk according to the same vision. This will eventually make every member a leader who is capable of efficiently training disciples (2 Tim. 3:16,17).

13. Visualize the Ministerial Network. Start to talk about it and pray about it. Ask God for guidance so He can show you who your leaders will be and when they will be appointed.

Existing Churches in Other Cell Systems

If a church is deeply involved in a traditional cell structure, the implementation strategy will be slightly different. The G-12 vision should be introduced and operated parallel to whatever system the church is currently using. As the G-12 vision starts to develop momentum, it will slowly collapse the supervisory levels of the traditional cell system. Eventually, it will absorb the entire traditional system into the G-12 vision. No cells need to be abandoned — only given permission to consolidate into the G-12 models.

Many pastors think they have a church working within the model of the G-12. But the truth is, they barely have Multiplication Cells. A G-12 structure has been formed only when people have conquered the primordial or fundamental methods of evangelization through cells and/or the consolidation process.

A good way to check yourself is your budget. If you spend more money on the Celebration Services than you do on cells, you still don't have the G-12 vision. Keep balanced, and each will cause growth in the other.

Multiplication Cells vs. Family Groups

Churches already working within the cell vision will have to adapt to the G-12 vocabulary. Family Groups, Home Encounters, Home Groups, Home Church, Communion Groups, or other similar names used for cells should be rejected in favor of calling the small groups Multiplication Cells. Multiplication Cells is a more appropriate name for cell meetings held in every setting.

When cell groups are called "Family Group meetings," they often put more emphasis on the communion of the faithful than on evangelization. Everyone should be involved in evangelization, saving lives in their geographical space, in their arenas of life, and in their own spheres of influence, such as at home, at work, at school, or with their friends. Other names also lessen the understanding that a healthy "cell" is part of a body and never a "stand-alone" entity.

The Transition Phase In a Church With No Family or Cell Groups

When a church does not work with Family Groups, Multiplication Cells must first be implemented, making cells out of the entire church so new people can be won to the Lord.

When this vision is implemented in an already existing church, it becomes necessary for that church to go through a transition phase. During this phase, not everyone is going to jump in right away. Church members willing to embrace the vision will go through the Encounter. Those first brave souls will make up the initial group; the rest will follow. Some will leave the church, however, not wanting their sins exposed.

The primary goal in this phase is to get as many people as possible to experience an Encounter. This will heal most of the problems that are holding the church back from growth. During the Encounters, the vision will be given for the groups of 12. The intensity of the Encounter provides an excellent environment in which to share the G-12 vision.

After the Encounters, the hunt for the 12 breaks loose. Certainly, this will be a time of adjustment for those who are more mature in the church. However, in the beginning, none will have a G-12. Everyone starts with a Multiplication Cell, even the senior pastor. Having passed the transition phase, the church now starts to fill its cells with new believers, and the vision takes off running!

With Whom Do We Share the Vision?

The G-12 vision should never be shared with someone who doesn't want to hear it. (This principle doesn't always hold true when sharing the Gospel, but soulwinning and church government are two different things.) If a local church or ministry doesn't receive the vision, the Lord simply takes it away from them. The vision must be shared only with people who can at least appreciate it and show a sincere interest in getting to learn more about it.

People who are merely curious will often give unsolicited and possibly destructive criticism. Therefore, make the vision special by sharing it only with trusted servants in the beginning. Once the vision takes hold, the momentum of success will help it gain acceptance.

For us to achieve success in this vision, we have to be obedient to the Master's Word and share the vision with open-minded people. We want the nobility of what has been entrusted to us to be truthfully received and passed on. The model of 12 isn't only understood through the method, but even more so through the anointing.

Who Stays in Your G-12

The time will come when the only ones remaining in your G-12 are those bearing fruit. Fruit-bearing is the key. It all depends on the fruit. If someone shows a rebellious attitude and produces more trouble than results, that person cannot remain on the front line. It is necessary that every single one of the 12 has an irreproachable character. If the senior pastor's group of 12 is well guarded and trained, all the other generations will be well-fed and healthy. This is true for every G-12. Every leader should regard his cell with just as much importance as the G-12 of the senior pastor.

What To Do When a Person Is Not Bearing Fruit in a G-12

Jesus did not reject any of the 12, but some removed themselves in His moment of need. This made it necessary for Jesus to restore them after His resurrection, as was the case of Peter (Mark 16:7; John 21).

If the lifestyle or behavior of a person in your cell starts giving a bad testimony, ask him to leave the G-12; then begin a disciplinary process in a "special" cell. Discipline corrects and puts the fear of God in a person's heart, which keeps the G-12 healthy. There is no true love without correction; on the other hand, every correction must be done in love. Be firm when necessary, but never lose tenderness.

In Summary

Start with a plan of what you want to accomplish and stick with it. Select your team carefully and keep the vision "out there" all the time.

A cell-oriented church is a ministry that embraces and understands the vision of Jesus Christ for conquering the nations. Jesus started His ministry with a team of 12 men (Mark 3:13-19). After giving these 12 men specialized training, Jesus delegated authority to them and anointed them so they would spread the Gospel and increase His Kingdom throughout the whole world.

A cell-oriented church continues this principle, beginning with a discipler who loves the vision. The discipler generates a group of 12 disciples, who will generate thousands of other disciples of like characteristics and quality (Phil. 3:17).

There is much more to be implemented in the cell vision and the groups of 12. The vision bears much fruit, and will bring great structural and organizational challenges. But the Lord is good and will give us His grace for everything He expects us to carry out (Phil. 2:13-18).

How To Conduct Successful Cell Meeting
Chapter 13

A specific and effective pattern has been developed for conducting successful cell meetings, which I will show you later in this chapter. First, however, I want to take you through the "Ten Commandments of the G-12 Cell Vision." If these ten basic guidelines are followed, your success in fulfilling the vision is virtually guaranteed!

The Ten Commandments Of the G-12 Cell Vision

1. LOVE THE VISION

First Corinthians 13 stimulates us to reproduce God's life through love. That is why it is important to love the ministry. It is clear there cannot be fruit without love (Col. 3:14).

The Multiplication Cells must be established in our hearts. We must live and breathe the vision, which is that every person realizes all God has for him or her with respect to ministry. We should want all people to receive everything God has for them, both now and in the hereafter. Our mission is the multiplication of saints through this model of 12. Our desire is that all will participate in this vision, sharing the same language.

The divine call is not for us to compete, but rather to *multiply* (Phil. 2:3). Therefore, we must not allow competition between disciples, Multiplication Cells, G-12s, Ministry Networks, or Supporting Groups (such as praise and worship, prayer and intercession, arts, etc.). We are all going for the same goal — the increase of the Kingdom of God.

2. DO NOT TURN AWAY (BE DISTRACTED) FROM THE VISION

The vision is to *Win*, *Consolidate*, *Disciple*, and *Send*. It includes the following principles:

• Multiplication Cells satisfy numerical growth through multiplication.
• The goal is the fulfillment of the Great Commission.
• The G-12s satisfy personal edification, achieving maturity of the saints and helping them change into the image of Christ Jesus.
• The G-12 vision is merely a return to the strategy Jesus had for making disciples.

Cells must not grow fat; if they do, they will turn away from the vision and stagnation will set in. This inactivity will get them off course. When a cell becomes idle, you can compare it with stagnant water, which eventually becomes smelly and is poisonous. Likewise, cell groups need to be constantly in motion so they will multiply themselves.

Cells are the spinal column of the ministry; everything revolves around them. The vision of the church creates a foundation for the cells, which must work to carry out the vision. The cells must not have a separate agenda; they are only to embrace and support the overall vision set forth by the church.

In addition, each cell needs to work with a specific vision or plan that allows it to achieve its goals of multiplication. The cell vision might simply be to belong to one of the Ministry Networks, or it could be something more unique. The important point here is that vision *builds unity*.

We have only one model, one vision, and one principle: *Win, Consolidate, Disciple,* and *Send*. We must not acknowledge any other system or course of action that is different from the one that has been adopted. If there is more than one vision, there will be division and, eventually, death to the G-12 system. Therefore, everything must promote the health of the cells. Don't depart from the vision!

3. DO NOT ALLOW THE CELLS TO BE UNFRUITFUL

Every disciple needs to evangelize. Every disciple is a believer carrying out his purpose to multiply himself. Therefore, even if a leader has a successful G-12, he must continue to look for new souls to be won. This is the leader's purpose (Matt. 28:18-20) — to take his disciples outside the four walls of the church so they can go and preach the Gospel (Mark. 16:15).

However, the leader should always keep in mind that the only way to achieve true results with this multiplication process is to *begin with prayer and fasting.*

4. HOLD AT LEAST ONE MEETING PER WEEK

A cell meeting should be held every week to solidify the vision and stimulate multiplication. Every meeting needs to have a strong evangelistic appeal, inspiring and motivating the disciples to win souls.

During the six days preceding each meeting, everyone in the cell will labor for the souls of the lost through prayer and fasting. When new people come to the Multiplication Cells, they will receive Jesus as their Lord and Savior because prayer has already covered them. Each cell must pursue the goal of saving souls. The church must never deviate from that purpose.

5. USE THE CELLS FOR RESTORING FAMILIES

We find family crises occurring all over the world. Cells are the answers to those problems. If we want to find solutions in these difficult matters, we must possess a wise and discerning spirit (Eph. 1:17).

Cell ministry brings the family to God by bringing God to the family. Because the church is in the home, it will be easier to discern the problem, heal the wounds, and break the chains of the past and the ties of hereditary curses (Exod. 20:5).

6. MAKE EACH MEMBER A LEADER

The key to the success of the G-12 vision is the premise that every person is a leader. It might take years to uncover leadership ability in some people; nevertheless, that ability is there.

When we in the ministry treat everyone like a winner, they become what we say, just as God changed Abram's name to Abraham, and Jesus changed Simon's name to Peter. In each case, God called these men what they were not so they could become what He said (Rom. 4:17).

God gave us authority over the animals, elements, and circumstances of this world, but not over other people. Since that is the case, everyone must be capable of operating in some level of leadership.

7. USE CELLS TO PROMOTE HOLINESS

Through accountability, which naturally occurs within the fellowship of a cell group, all cell members are called upon to live and walk in holiness (1 Thess. 4:3,4; 1 Peter 1:16). Leaders must insist on ministering to people in such a way as to help them attain holiness. The wages of sin is death (Rom. 6:23); therefore, sin must be immediately confessed and forsaken (Ps. 32:5). If sin creeps unchecked into a cell, it will die.

8. DO NOT WORK ON ANOTHER'S GROUND

We should not try to draw in someone from another ministry or church. *People from other churches are not the target group!* The vision calls for evangelization, not theft.

Also, every one of our members must be true to his group and not change from one discipler to another. If a problem should arise in the group, we must treat the situation appropriately, without transferring it to someone else.

9. NEVER GIVE PLACE TO MURMURING, COMPLAINING, OR GOSSIP

In cell meetings, we cannot permit gossip about pastors, leaders, or directors. If any leader has a deficiency or problem, prayer is the only solution; backbiting won't help at all. We must be radical in this endeavor, never permitting any gossip or negative, malicious comments from disciples in the cell at any time.

10. BE FAITHFUL IN ACHIEVING GOALS

Realistic goals must be set for both growth and evangelism. Any goal that does not have a date attached to it is not a realistic one, but rather a fantasy. It is therefore necessary to be rational, establishing well-designed and achievable goals in search of realistic multiplication.

It is desirable to set both short-term and long-term goals. One goal per year can be set. Don't wait until the end of the year to evaluate your progress. Divide the year into four stages, evaluating each stage at the end of the quarter and making the necessary adjustments.

Meeting Dynamics

THE TIME

The time of the cell meeting is best set by the cell members. For most people, this seems to be after work. For others, the needs are best met at noon or early in the morning. Let the leaders decide what works best for them and their cell members. *It is important not to restrict cell meetings to any particular day or time, other than avoiding regularly scheduled church services.*

After determining the time of day to hold the cell meeting, the leader needs to decide what day. As noted above, he should make sure it isn't held at a time when there is a regularly scheduled church event, such as Sunday mornings. This would interfere with the local body as a whole and could prove to be disruptive. Whenever church programs compete against cell meetings, the cells should always defer because by their nature, they are subordinate to the church. To repeat: Church-sponsored activities generally take precedent over any cell activities.

You must remember that the cell and the church are not in competition. This is where many have failed in implementing a cell-oriented government. They have pitted the church against itself by trying to run church programs and cells at the same time. If the church is not careful, it will choke out the very thing that is strengthening and consolidating it.

In order to eliminate competition, many churches have canceled mid-week and even Sunday night services in favor of cell meetings. For many pastors, canceling a well-attended midweek service is painful. But we must not forget that the goal is to make disciples of all nations — not just to "have church." If cells do a better job at making disciples, a decision to cancel a service in favor of cell meetings could prove more profitable in the long run. And don't worry about the offerings. People get paid weekly, bimonthly, or monthly.

Because cell meetings are held in homes, a visitor arriving an hour early can catch a housewife unprepared. It can also cause a very uncomfortable situation if the visitor happens to be a single male arriving before the husband gets home or the other guests arrive. The reverse can also happen and is just as undesirable. One solution is to place a few chairs outside for early arrivers, just in case.

To help train everyone to be on time, start on time, no matter how many people are there. If you wait until everyone shows up, you will find the meetings getting pushed back later and later. It is very important that everyone strive to be on time for the meetings.

THE LOCATION

Location is key to the success of any meeting. When and where a meeting takes place is of vital importance, especially before the cell consolidates into a G-12. The meeting place must lend itself to the new visitor, making it as accessible as possible.

Most cell literature recommends that a cell meeting be held in different locations each week. My experience is different, however. Oftentimes, changing locations every week can lead to confusion and missed opportunities for the new people. Until the cell consolidates into the fraternal group of 12, it seems best to commit to having the meeting at a fixed time and place every week. Once the meeting closes or consolidates into a G-12, it can then become more flexible, meeting when and where it best suits the needs of the group.

For many reasons, it is almost always better to have the meeting in the home of someone other than the leader. This principle guarantees that at least two families will be involved. It is also a way of sharing responsibilities.

The beauty of the cell group is that it happens where the people are — outside the church. The church building or sanctuary often intimidates people. Would a sinner want to come to God's house and be faced with guilt and condemnation? No! Getting a person to church can be a monumental task due to the guilt related to sin and the spiritual implications of a church building. On the other hand, a cell group is much less intimidating and threatening. It isn't God's house; it's a neighbor's house or a place of employment. The bottom line is that it is more "user friendly," less intimidating, and easier to escape from if necessary.

ROOM ENVIRONMENT

The single most important factor in the "meeting place" dynamics is the position of the chairs. I know this sounds elementary, but chair placement has a major effect on the success or failure of a meeting. It is for this very reason that, before official political negotiations start, someone evaluates and determines the size of the room, the shape of the table, and the positioning of the chairs.

Where and how people sit has a lot to do with how they relate to the others in the group. The seating arrangement should be circular if possible. All the seats should never be facing a speaker, as in a classroom or church setting.

The idea is that all seats should point toward the middle, facing each other rather than the speaker. Remember, it is not a teaching session, nor is it a classroom environment. It is a "Holy Ghost huddle" — a family gathering. The leader is not sitting at the head or in front, but in the same ring with the others.

The goal is to have a seating arrangement in which each person feels comfortable when speaking. The leader is to be more of a quarterback than a coach. All are in the cell process together. Each family participates in the success of the whole— that is, each member helps the others in the group become conformed to the image of Christ.

The lighting at the meeting is also very important. Each person should have enough light to read if necessary. It is not a good idea to have people read in rounds or out loud. Many people were traumatized in school by having to read out loud; consequently, it is oftentimes very stressful for some adults to do so. The leader should therefore learn who likes to read and ask these members to read at the appropriate time, taking turns if necessary.

Even though optimum situations are desirable, they are not always possible. Don't worry if the space is too small for the chairs to form a perfect circle, if the house or job site is not climate-controlled, or if the lighting is poor. In Bolivia, where I pastor, most meetings are held outside in the dirt or on the porch where people sit on benches. A single 40-watt fluorescent bulb provides the light. It is the love of God shining through the cell members that draws in the people.

Love is what spells success, not the chairs or the lighting. If we continue to lift Jesus higher, men will be drawn to Him (John 12:32). Our job as the undershepherds is to eliminate obstacles that would prevent sheep from coming to Christ.

To start off the meeting, it is nice to serve something to drink or offer a light snack. Neither is necessary, but having something light to drink and eat adds to the fellowship. It stimulates social contacts and especially helps relax the visitors. Providing food and drink may help an outsider blend in and keep them from feeling self-conscious.

CELL MINISTRY

Like church, cell meetings also have an order of service. As in a church service, this order is subject to the leading of the Holy Ghost. Any order, then, is actually an auxiliary agenda, ready to be implemented if it is not changed by the Holy Ghost.

It is very important to understand that all things should be subject to the Holy Ghost and that any "pattern" established by man must always be subject to His leading. Every church has its own personality, motivations, and gifts, all of which need to go into the cell meeting formula. It should be understood that the following cell pattern is one that has been proven successful by years of experience. Caution should be exercised, therefore, before deviating too far from its principles.

The following is the order of ministry in the cell: Encounter, Exaltation, Edification, Evangelism, and Teaching.

ENCOUNTER

The purpose of the cell meeting is to provide us with the opportunity to have an "encounter" with God. He is the only One who can change us; therefore, everyone in the meeting needs to have this encounter. If this purpose is fulfilled, we'll also have an encounter with our cell brothers and our leader. A meeting is of little use if this primary purpose hasn't been achieved. Therefore, an encounter with God for all who are present is the first objective.

EXALTATION

The way to experience the Presence of God is through praise, worship, thanksgiving, and prayer. It is impossible to have an encounter with God without exalting Him. As people focus on Him, they will be impacted with His love, and the meeting will be filled with His glory.

The Name of Jesus Christ must be exalted constantly (Phil. 2:9, 10), not because God needs our praise, but because we can then enjoy the blessings that emanate from praising and worshiping Him. A gifted guitar player can usher a small group into the throne room of God and be a tremendous blessing. Even a novice can help harmonize a group, leading them in worship.

If no one in the group is a musician who can lead the group in worship, the group can always sing along with a music cassette or CD. Don't be afraid to sing *a cappella* — without any instrumental guidance. If the group's hearts are sincere, their praise will always sound beautiful to God.

A great time to pray is right after worship while the group is still in an atmosphere of praise. Allow anyone who wants to pray to step right in and make his or her request known to God. In some circles, everyone prays at the same time, whereas others prefer taking turns to pray. It really doesn't matter how the group does it. What matters is that a relaxed and anointed atmosphere prevails as they pray to their Heavenly Father.

Prayer that follows worship can be the most special time of the week. When prayer flows, it can be tremendously anointed. Experiences such as this in the Presence of God are what keep men and women coming back week after week.

However, if the only time the group members pray or worship is during the cell meeting or in church, their attempt to enter into the Presence of God will be dry and unfruitful. The cell leader should therefore strongly encourage members to pray and worship at home, as well as in the cell meetings.

The time and location of a meeting will influence the type of worship that is appropriate. For instance, if the meeting is being held in a public place such as a restaurant or job site, the cell members may not have the liberty to sing with the same boldness and intensity they might exhibit in a private home.

The length of the meeting is also a determining factor. For example, if the meeting is only supposed to last an hour, 45 minutes of worship will not leave much time to do anything else. For a normal meeting of an hour and a half, a typical worship session should last 15 to 20 minutes.

Worshiping God can be defined as any act that brings people into His Presence. Without the Presence of God in your cell meetings, you will have nothing more than a social gathering, and it will be very difficult to experience a sense of unity during that meeting. The least you should expect from a time of worship is unity. Singing or worshiping together brings the group together in spirit. Therefore, your goal in worship should always be unity with God and with fellow cell group members.

EDIFICATION

This seems to be the portion of a cell meeting that is most misunderstood and most feared by pastors. It also intimidates most potential cell leaders. You see, one of the biggest mistakes people make in regard to cell systems is to think of a cell group meeting as a Bible study. A cell meeting is never a Bible study. It is a people study using the Bible.

For whatever reason, the concept that a cell meeting is a Bible study seems to be a difficult one to dispel. Generally, the cell will start to bloom once the leaders understand that the cell is not a mini-church or a group of people trying to figure out what the Bible means. There is no pulpit nor no formality at the cell meeting. Rather, the cell is the Christian community broken down to its smallest fighting unit, similar to a platoon in an army. Obviously, individual families are even smaller units, but if families stand alone, they are vulnerable. The cell puts family units together so they can successfully stand against the wiles of the devil.

Again, a cell meeting is not a teaching session. It is a time of sharing personal life experiences based on the Word. The reason why some pastors don't like cells and choose not to participate is they fear that a charismatic or gifted teacher will begin to draw people to himself and away from them. The reason most potential cell leaders are intimidated is that they feel unprepared to deal with tough questions or difficult situations.

The solution to both of these situations requires a little preparation on the pastor's part. A simple outline can be given to the Multiplication Cell leaders to provide that gifted or charismatic teacher with some parameters. It will also help preserve the vision of the church, keeping the topics of discussion under the pastor's control. Writing such an outline also provides help in message preparation, thus giving confidence to an inexperienced leader.

I have found it very helpful to publish the cell topic in the bulletin or to announce it from the pulpit. This serves to ensure that the targeted topic will be the only one used by the leaders.

The G-12 structure stands superior to the other models in that each disciple hears the week's topic discussed before he presents it to *his* disciples. The senior pastor meets first with his group. The same subject the senior pastor ministers on in his cell meeting is then discussed in the meetings of the other G-12s (2 Tim. 2:2). Through a chain of command, the information is passed from one group to another. This leaves little room for error or intimidation.

It is important to remember that there are two kinds of cells in the G-12 structure: Multiplication Cells and Edification Cells. The G-12 is an Edification Cell. Therefore, what the senior pastor shares in his G-12 meeting is almost never the topic for groups that have yet to consolidate, or for Multiplication Cells. Multiplication Cells have a separate curriculum that takes each group through the basics, guiding it into consolidation, or into a G-12 cell.

When meeting with his disciples, the discipler shouldn't allow questions that cause confusion or that distract from the content (1 Cor. 14:40). Providing copies of the lessons to participants will save time and will also guarantee that the vision will be passed on unmodified from the first to the last disciple.

In the G-12 model, the delivery is a highly effective, interactive communication system — a system just like Jesus used. The ability of the G-12 system to deliver a message is so efficient that it can stand alone; it doesn't need the Sunday message to support it.

The G-12 provides more discipline for the people than a lecture does. This system gets people off the pew and catapults them into the ministry, helping to move them into their destiny as ambassadors for Christ.

Every member of the Body of Christ is called to the ministry of reconciliation. Therefore, it is important that the disciples give testimonies of people whose lives they have touched. This will help keep them motivated to save souls (Isa. 52:7).

You must constantly stress to the congregation that they are in a church of revival. The main goal of the church is to save souls and, ultimately, to win your city for Jesus. Always remind your disciples that they are carrying out Isaiah 54:2, 3:

Enlarge the place of thy tent, and let them stretch forth the curtains of thine habitations: spare not, lengthen thy cords, and strengthen thy stakes;
For thou shalt break forth on the right hand and on the left; and thy seed shall inherit the Gentiles, and make the desolate cities to be inhabited.

Once the group consolidates and is closed to new members, the format shifts. At this point, helping the saints mature in their walk is priority.

Before a cell consolidates into a G-12, the leader deals largely with issues such as divorce, child or wife abuse, addictions, as well as other vices and sin — basically helping people out of the filth and rubbish of the world. After the cell has been consolidated, the emphasis changes from crisis management to character development. More time is spent on the gifts and fruit of the Spirit. The G-12 members concentrate on laying aside the weights that easily beset them so they can run their race and mature in Christ.

Once consolidated, the cell also shifts into a management team, helping the members organize the disciples of the next generation. This transition is a big reason why this system is so fulfilling to cell members. Instead of having to deal with the same problems week after week, the group moves up into administration.

To help you better understand how the G-12 system works, let's look at a sensitive topic such as tithing. Money is reported to be the number-one cause for offense in the Church. When a message on giving comes forth from the pulpit, even when it is presented with love and an anointing, it is often perceived as self-serving. On the other hand, in a cell meeting, the topic can be discussed in a way that eliminates objections and builds confidence in the pastor's vision.

In a cell meeting, the reasons for giving as presented in the Word can be reinforced by one's peers. A small-group discussion can potentially reveal why certain members of the group don't like to tithe and uncover hidden fears, doubts, and misunderstandings that some have about the promises of God. Many times the fires of rebellion and criticism are extinguished in the cell meeting before those destructive flames have a chance to spill out into the church at large.

Everyone should be encouraged to participate during the time devoted to the Word. A good leader will not only help direct the discussion of God's Word but will encourage introverts to speak out as well. An even greater challenge for the leader might be controlling the extroverts — keeping them silent long enough to give the others an opportunity to speak. The skill that leaders must develop is to get people to talk about how a certain passage of Scripture affects their lives without *interrupting them.*

If the cell leader happens to be a Greek scholar, that's great — but it provides no benefit to him as a cell leader. He can always use his talents as a teacher in a Bible school or college. However, the cell meeting is not necessarily the time to dig out heavy revelations from the Word. It is a time for cell members to share their lives with one another, holding each other accountable in brotherly love. This does not mean condemning or judging one another. Rather, it is an opportunity for the group members to share one another's joys, sorrows, necessities, and burdens.

Ministering God's Word enables the leader to motivate and edify the people in his group of 12 (Heb. 4:12; 2 Tim. 3:16, 17). It is important that he minister to the disciples he has chosen to be with him. They need to be strengthened by the Word. They need to understand that they are worthy. They need to understand that there are solutions to their problems. They need to be edified by the Word spoken through their leader.

Generally, we are receptive to sin and hostile to holiness; we inherited this trait from Adam. God was inflicted with pain when Adam sinned. The Hebrew text makes it clear to us that when God called out, *"Adam, where are you?"* He was feeling the pain of Adam's transgression. God knew where Adam was; it was Adam who didn't understand the position he had placed himself in (Gen. 3:8-11).

We were born with a sinful nature (Ps. 51:5); therefore, in order to remove this characteristic from us, we must indeed fight a spiritual battle and allow our inner man to be renewed and edified (2 Cor. 4:16).

To *edify* means "to build up." Christ's character has to be built up and developed first in us and then in our brothers through us (Eph. 4:13). When we receive edification, it causes us to denounce and confess sin and death; only then is the power of sin and death broken in our lives. When edification is evident, sin can no longer be disguised and all accounts are settled.

Everyone should leave every cell meeting edified. Christ is the Edifier of the Church, and Christ lives in us (Rom. 8:11). Edification brings health to the cell. An edified cell group will bear much fruit and multiply.

However, our lives cannot be edified when they are built on top of a foundation of sin. Sin needs to be confessed so there can be forgiveness (Ps. 32:5). We must not build walls around the enemy lurking inside our lives because, in doing so, we sleep with him.

EVANGELIZATION

It is very important that everyone attending feels welcome to the Multiplication Cell. The way the meeting begins will have a big effect on the visitors' ability to receive later on. During this "ice-breaking time," the host should be prepared with questions to ask or interesting topics to share. This helps to move people into a comfortable and relaxed atmosphere, which is crucial for a successful meeting.

The questions or discussions during the opening few moments should be kept light and unobtrusive. Even if they are low-profiled, each question should stimulate conversation and help people relax. This is not the time to put a visitor through the third degree. Don't pry or let others pry into visitors' private lives. Instead, let the visitors share their experiences with the group as they sense a leading to do so.

The cornerstone of this vision is evangelization; therefore, this element needs to be present in every Multiplication Cell. The testimonies of what God is doing through evangelization should always be part of the G-12 agenda.

The goal should be to establish Multiplication Cells in every part of the city so that, at any given time, a cell meeting is being held somewhere in the local area. To achieve that goal, the 12 need to be real evangelists who continually pursue this vision of getting the message of the Cross proclaimed at all times in all places.

Evangelization refers to our interest in taking each individual to the Cross and ministering to him the four spiritual laws:

- The need to recognize that he is a sinner.
- The need to know that death is the price to pay for sin.
- The need to know that the blood of Jesus purifies from sin.
- The need to receive Jesus Christ as Lord and Savior of his life.

Because Jesus died for us, the plan of salvation is indispensable in the Multiplication Cells. Everyone must know that Love went to the Cross of Calvary and died for them there.

We know what this means because we have taken up our own cross. Every day we need to go to the Cross of Christ, recognizing that we would be sinners who lack God's holiness if not for the fact that we are now in Him. Our old sin nature has passed away (2 Cor. 5:17); we are now partakers of Christ's nature (2 Peter 1:4).

It is also important to announce in the meetings that the person who has received Jesus has been granted the following rights as a child of God:

1. He can talk to the Father in prayer (John 1:12).

2. He can hear God's voice through His Word. Anyone who nurtures himself with the living Word of God will have eternal life, for Jesus is both the bread of life and living water (John 6:32-35).

When we are hungry, we buy food. It's the same for our spiritual life: We must look for spiritual food, which comes to us through God's Word.

Therefore, the new believer should be motivated to buy a Bible. Reading it will feed his spirit with the life that is in God's Word.

3. *He is part of a very special family — God's family.* Jesus says that we are brothers (Matt. 12:49; 23:8).

TEACHING

The best teachings are those we share with our lifestyle. When we fellowship closely with people, they will see our behavior and really get to know us.

Disciples don't learn from the printed page or from lectures as much as they learn from watching us "practice what we preach"— both by precept and example. We must not demand from others what we ourselves don't do. Disciples aren't made by mere words. It is necessary to walk the same road with the people we want to influence.

In the G-12s and in the Multiplication Cells, our testimony has to be alive in order for us to minister a life of quality to others We have to treat our disciples and the people around us in encouraging ways. As we love them, they will do the same when they have their own disciples.

Our teaching must be the byproduct of our living experience. It's easy to talk but not so easy to do. Jesus said that he who has the Word and does not put it into practice is ignorant and foolish. He is similar to the man who built his house on sand (Matt. 7:26).

In the midst of it all, we must not lose track of our Kingdom goals. Our G-12 slogan is *"Souls, Cells, Families."* We have to save souls; take them to the cells; and win their families.

Some Final Considerations

THE CLOSE OF THE MEETING

• It is always important to close any session in prayer. Because of time restrictions, it is usually better for one individual to pray. At the end of the meeting, every disciple should be mentioned and blessed in prayer. Also, the person praying should pray about any needs that have been shared or discussed, as well as for your local church and its needs.

• After prayer, the meeting should end by announcing the vision of the church, as well as the vision of the cell. Ending this way allows the meeting to close on an "up note." As part of the vision, any announcements about future activities can also be given. This provides the information those attending will need to plan for both cell and church activities.

• The discipler has to love each of his disciples as though they were his children, inviting them to his house as often as possible. This will generate trust and intimacy. To help your cell leaders get to know their disciples better, strengthen the communion and fellowship of the groups in the Multiplication Cells through meetings, trips, and fun outings.

• It is very important to reinforce the vision in the church every quarter through a Cell Conference, an event that engages all the members.

• Dream big. A large church can impact a city — even a nation — more effectively than a small church can.

• Never think that you are standing alone. God will raise up "Joshuas" and "Calebs" to conquer the world with you (Josh. 1:3).

• Prepare yourself to receive other local and national leaders desiring to know the reason for the growth of your church. Take care of them and transmit God's vision (2 Tim. 2:1-2).

• Travel to Cell Conferences to find out what is going on in other places.

ADMINISTRATION

Another very positive aspect about the G-12 as a governing system is the small amount of paperwork required to make it work. All data in a G-12 is passed on to the management team above it. Cell information is passed up the line so that those in supervision will know everyone's place. Absences are monitored to help bring former members back into the fold.

Once a cell closes in the G-12 system, it moves from evangelism to discipleship. In the process, it becomes much easier to monitor. Evangelism is not lost; it is multiplied 12 times!

Summary of a Successful G-12 Cell Meeting

MULTIPLICATION CELL (Total time: 90 minutes)

• Ice-breaker — 10 minutes
• Encounter through exaltation and prayer — 20 minutes
• Edification — 45 minutes
• Evangelism motivation — 10 minutes
• Imparting of the vision and announcements — 5 minutes

G-12 (Total time: 1_ to 2 hours)

• Fellowship — 10 minutes
• Encounter through exaltation and prayer — 20 minutes
• Edification and teaching — 45 minutes

- Administration of disciples' cells — 30 minutes
- Evangelism — 10 minutes
- Imparting of the vision and announcements — 5 minutes

How the Children Fit In

The prophecy in Luke 1:17 (also found in Malachi 4:5,6) is vital for us if we want to participate in the last-day revival:

And he shall go before him in the spirit and power of Elias, to turn the hearts of the fathers to the children, and the disobedient to the wisdom of the just; to make ready a people prepared for the Lord.

As Christians, we all need to be family-oriented. Our children are part of the Body of Christ, and we need to treat them that way. Jesus instructed us in Matthew 19:14: *"...Suffer little children, and forbid them not, to come unto me: for of such is the kingdom of heaven."* That's why I stress that children must participate in cell meetings. They should be present when the adults meet together, even if they are in another room.

Any activity that does not allow children to participate is a respecter of persons and against the Word of God. "Children Not Allowed" is the sign the abortionists hang out. "All Children Welcome" should be the banner waving for any Christian activity. By not allowing children, we often exclude single mothers and wives with children whose husbands are out of town. Personally, I have fond and precious memories of moments when adults spoke into my life and allowed me to participate with them when I was young.

The words of the famous healing evangelist, Smith Wigglesworth, point out the importance of our ministry to children. He once said, "I just prayed with three and a half people to get saved."

The man to whom Wigglesworth was talking responded, "Three adults and a child?"

"No, Sir," Wigglesworth said. "Three children and an adult!" He went on to reason that the three children still had their whole lives in front of them, and the adult only had half his life left.

Children's ministry is one of the most overlooked areas. McDonald's has produced the largest food chain in history by marketing to children. When McDonald's started directing its advertising at children, the critics said it would never work. They said, "Kids have no money and no means of transportation." Fifty zillion hamburgers later, who was right? Marketing directed at children works!

As a pastor, I do all I can to promote children's ministry, because I know it reinforces the entire family. It builds both the local church and the Body of Christ.

Let's read Romans 12:2 as it relates to children's ministry: *"And be not conformed to this world: but be ye transformed by the renewing of your mind, that ye may prove what is that good, and acceptable, and perfect, will of God."* I know this verse has been given different interpretations, but we'll go with the interpretation that says there are varying degrees of perfection in our walk with God, with "good" being the least degree and "perfect" being the greatest. That leaves "acceptable" somewhere between the two.

The "good" way to involve the children in a cell meeting is to have a separate room for them where they can be entertained either by themselves or by a babysitter. This is better than leaving the children at home because it allows them to participate, even if it is only by being there. If you are dealing with minimum experience and commitment, backyard games with supervision is fun for children, and it keeps them away from the parents so they can minister to one another.

The "perfect" way to involve the children is to rotate group members (each one taking part) in a scheduled Bible study with the children. Determining whether to adopt the "good, acceptable, or perfect" method many times has to do more with experience in ministry than with desire. I might add that any method is only "perfect" in theory because only Jesus is perfect in practice. So we might say this last method is the most mature way — the least selfish and the most fulfilling. "Perfect" is always the goal, but it is not always obtainable.

In the perfect system, every group member — including the leader — teaches the children. After leading the children in a time of praise and worship, the teacher uses a fully developed curriculum that incorporates a systematic study of the Bible while giving the children fun and exciting things to do that cultivate their interest in God and His Word. A rotation of teachers assures that all the adults participate in the care and ministry of the children. This both increases the adults' experience in ministry and helps them get to know each other's children as they utilize their own gifts and talents.

You might be surprised how much a brief conversation with a child can reveal about what is going on in his home. Parents who don't want to bring their children to the cell meetings might be afraid that the children will reveal what they are hiding. Thus, teaching the Word to the children offers the opportunity to minister both to the children and the parents.

The "acceptable" way to involve children in a cell meeting can be found somewhere between the "good" and the "perfect." In the acceptable category are options such as one person in the group teaching the children every week or the children participating in simple activities such as coloring pictures in a Christian coloring book.

"Good" is a lot better than nothing, but "acceptable" is one step closer to "perfect." "Acceptable" includes any options that are more than just babysitting but not yet a full-blown curriculum. Perhaps the group pays a teenager or accepts a volunteer to not only care for the children, but to also minister to them in some way.

The difficulty in this is that many times, there is a diverse group of children to minister to. The method that has worked well in my cell group is to have the older children play with the younger ones. An adult then reads Bible stories to the children as they color pictures. This method makes it possible to minister to a wide range of ages.

There are several ministries that offer great children's materials. Your Christian beliefs and doctrine will determine where you go for your material. Standard Sunday school material will work fine.

Remember, if your cell meeting follows the pattern established in this book, the children are only away from the parents for 45 to 60 minutes. And no matter where you are in your children's cell ministry, the children can always participate in the praise and worship. A normal five-year-old can stand or sit and participate in praise and worship with the adults.

I have found the cell group to be a great place to discover who is disciplining their children and who isn't. It amazes me to see powerful men and women of God ordered around by their four-year-old children!

As a pastor, I know that there are often "untouchable" areas in people's lives, and money and children are two of the most guarded ones. But if the babies are running the house, that home is not in order. If the children are out of control, the home is out of control as well.

It is not acceptable for the parents to leave their children at home because that leaves the children out of the cell group experience. The cell is a community of believers, and the children are a part of that community. I sometimes hear that the children are the Church of tomorrow. That is wrong! They are the Church of *today*!

For a cell to accomplish all it must do, provision must be made for the children. Leaving them at home is not the solution. However, with four children of my own, I know parents are often tempted to do just that.

The cell group also shouldn't leave out the babysitter. In the "good" or the "acceptable" scenarios I have just described, one person could possibly be taking care of everyone's children. That means that only one babysitter is left out of the group discussion, causing the entire group to benefit from that person's presence as all the other adults participate in the cell meeting.

Sometimes a teenager who has his or her own cell group can work in this manner for another group. This works especially well in a new cell group where attendance is still small, and no one wants to miss out by being with the children.

A SPECIAL NOTE: Keeping the men's meetings separate from the women's meetings allows the parent not at the meeting to stay home with the children. Separating the genders to form homogenous groups is one great solution to the children question. That is one reason it is recommended that, if the senior pastor is married, both he and his wife lead separate G-12 groups.

Group Dynamics
Chapter 14

In this chapter, I want to examine the basics of relationships within a cell group setting. Relationships are the essence, the "backbone," of the quality of our lives. Whether we are single, married, divorced, widowed, or somewhere in between, our relationships and friendships are what give meaning to our lives.

Moms, dads, brothers, sisters, friends, coworkers, teachers, students, bosses, roommates, employees, teammates — all these are people with whom we have relationships. Yet in all those relationships, "challenge" is their middle name! There has never been, nor will there ever be, a relationship free of challenges.

How do we cope with relationship problems? Volumes have been written on this subject. Since the days of Adam and Eve, human beings have been trying to gain insight into how they can improve their relationships. And ever since Adam and Eve, human beings have had a tough time of it!

After Adam and Eve sinned in the Garden of Eden, people have had great difficulty in their relationship with God. In Genesis 3:11 and 12, when God asked Adam the critical question about whether he had eaten the forbidden fruit from the tree, Adam admitted that he had, but he put the blame on Eve. Eve also made excuses for eating the fruit, blaming the serpent (v. 13).

Since that day, relationships between two or more people and between people and God have been troublesome. The truth is, if you are married, have children, or have a job, you have challenges in one or more of those relationships.

Why all the trouble in relationships? Part of the problem is that we humans are so wonderfully complex. Not only do we have trillions of cells fusing us into a biochemical matrix called flesh, but we are also spiritual beings who are formed into the likeness of an enormously complex God. No saint has ever had a neat little life. Apostles Peter and Paul had relationship problems, as did many other people in the Bible. Everyone needs help in improving their relationships.

The Importance of Relationships

In the Chinese language, whole words are written with a symbol. Often, two completely different symbols used together have a meaning quite different than either one of the components used alone. For example, the symbols for "man" and for "woman," when combined, mean "good." Similarly, the symbol for "trouble" and "gathering crisis" are combined to mean "opportunity."

When we think about it, these concept combinations make sense. As the answers to life always lie in the questions, so the opportunities of life lie in our problems.

Some people have strong, loving relationships with people around them who support and enhance their lives. Others have experienced a complete breakdown in communication in their most important relationships, such as their relationship with their spouse.

Whereas relationships add great richness to our lives, they can also add great pain. Within our relationships exist some of life's most complex and painful problems.

The Basics

Here are four simple ideas to consider when wrestling with relational problems within the cell.

1. **First**, we should never bring up a challenging topic without having already prepared a solution to the problem. Many times we spend much of our time responding or reacting to problems in a relationship rather than finding out the true cause of those problems. Another way we mishandle problems is by talking about them with others, gossiping and complaining rather than working together in love. If we would just take the time to find out the cause of a relationship problem, we could then creatively work toward a solution.

2. **Second**, when describing a relational problem, we shouldn't just say that the other person is a jerk. That only labels the person and makes problem-solving more difficult. Instead, define the exact actions of the person that bother you and then go from there.

3. **Third**, beware of "either/or" categories. Saying that someone is either stupid or a fool doesn't do any good for anyone. Let's not desire to be right so badly that we lose the ability to solve the problem. A win/lose situation usually means that both parties will eventually lose. Try to work out a win/win situation whenever possible.

4. **Fourth**, each of us is 100-percent responsible for all our relational difficulties. This may seem like a shocking thing to say, but it is true nevertheless.

This principle was shocking to me the first time I heard it. A friend of mine and his wife were going through great difficulties, which eventually led to their divorce. I was spending much time with my friend, trying to listen and help him. My wife shocked me by saying, *"That man will never even begin to solve his problems with his wife until he realizes that it is 100 percent his fault."* I quickly came to his defense, spouting the wife's problem areas. At that, my wife informed me that the wife was also 100 percent responsible for the relationship problems!

Too often, we think our relationships in terms of percentages, such as 50/50, 60/40, or even 70/30. In reality, however, the mathematics of relationships are really 100 percent/100 percent. Going halfway has never been God's solution for a problem in a relationship. Each of us is totally responsible for the relationship because the only person we can change is ourselves.

If you want to help your spouse, your child, your friend, or whomever, work on the problems rather than the symptoms. Recognize that the only person you have the power to change is yourself. Nothing is a greater obstacle to establishing good relationships than being dissatisfied with yourself.

If you want more passion and zest in your life, put more energy into changing yourself and developing your relationship with God. Relying solely on others to provide your passion will only result in frustration.

Self-love is a concept too often confused with vanity and pride. We think it's selfish to love ourselves, when in reality it is selfish *not* to. When we don't love ourselves, we take from others in order to fill our own emptiness.

It is important for us to realize that the better we feel about ourselves, the better we will feel about our relationships. All our relationships with people begin with our relationship with God. Christ has shown Himself among us; God has made His dwelling place within us. That fact sets us free to love each other. Unfortunately, too often we expect others to provide our peace, security, and love. In reality, however, these blessings come only from the Kingdom of God dwelling within us.

DON'T BLAME OTHERS

The only person I cannot help is the one who blames others. When a person blames others, he makes it difficult, if not impossible, to solve his own problems.

When relationship problems invade our lives, we must resist the temptation to accuse the other person. We must also learn not to blame ourselves and especially not to blame God. In order to figure out the source of a relationship problem, we must focus on *the problem* and not the other person. If there have been failures on either side, we must *confess* them within ourselves and *forgive* them in the other person. We have to put the problem in perspective so we can get on with problem-solving.

CONFLICT IS OPPORTUNITY

Conflict doesn't cause problems in relationships; rather, problems evolve from how we respond or react in conflict. We can choose to respond in one of two ways — either in self-defense or by choosing to simply learn from the experience.

When conflict arises in one of your relationships, ask yourself if you are trying to defend and protect yourself, or if you're trying to learn from this experience. Seeing conflict as an opportunity rather than a calamity puts it into a new and better light. You may think this sounds ridiculous, if not impossible, but you must face emotional pain willingly. It makes sense that when you stop blaming others and assume responsibility for your own life, change becomes possible.

Our relational problem-solving will always be unsuccessful as long as our primary interest is to protect ourselves. Problems will be solved and we will be changed if we commit ourselves to openness and learning.

DEAL WITH REAL ISSUES

The Western world has been programmed very narrowly. We have been taught to define problems, seek solutions, set goals, make decisions, and fix things. This quick-fix method includes fixing our spouse, our children, or ourselves. When we see something we don't like, we judge it and want to change it rather than understand it. We look for immediate solutions instead of seeking to understand how and why the problem arose in the first place.

This is why most relational problems never really get solved; they are just accepted. It is true that hiding from problems is easier than facing them, but avoiding problems will never get them solved.

There will never be "an appropriate time" to solve a relational problem. Therefore, deal with your problem now — don't wait. The Bible says not to let the sun go down on your anger (Eph. 4:26).

You must recognize when you have a relationship problem and find the first available moment to discuss it and confront it while it is still new. Problems are like food; left too long, they will not only grow stale, but will also begin to mold.

The best technique I know for solving and eliminating relationship problems is to spend time openly and honestly sharing your feelings with the person(s) involved. However, if you are having a problem with a member of your cell, meet privately with them. Never discuss the problem in front of the group.

LISTEN

Love is a four-letter word spelled t-i-m-e. The way you show someone you care for him is to spend time with him, listening intently to what he has to say.

One of the best ways to demonstrate God's love is to listen to people. Listening is the key to quality cell leadership. People feel good when someone is listening to them. When cell members know they have been heard, they will leave the meeting feeling satisfied and will look forward to coming to the next meeting. That is exactly why a cell group meeting is not a Bible study. It is not a time for the leader to speak, but to *listen*. A good leader encourages others to speak so they can feel satisfied and fulfilled.

The word "communication" comes from the Latin root *communus*, meaning, "to have something in common." Communication breaks down most often as a result of our inability or unwillingness to listen. According to a study in *U.S. News & World Report*, the single biggest reason couples split up is the inability to talk honestly with each other, to bare their souls, and to treat each other as their best friend.

You may be surprised to learn that listening is the most important key to communication. Professor H. W. Jurgen, a West German sociologist, claims that couples chat with each other for 70 minutes a day in their first year of marriage, dropping to 30 minutes in their second year and then to only 15 in their fourth. His research shows that by the eighth year, a husband and wife hardly share any small talk at all and become nearly silent.

Shocking? Not really, when you consider the findings of American science professor Ray Birdwhitsell, which I discovered in a Christian publication a few years ago. His studies show that American couples talk with each other for only 27.2 minutes a week. That's a daily ration of less than four minutes a day!

However, communication involves much more than words. One authority quoted in this publication said that only 7 percent of our communication involves the spoken word; another 38 percent is conveyed by body language, including gestures and facial expressions; and 55 percent is conveyed by the tone of our voice.

Listening is perhaps the most profound way we demonstrate to others that we love them. Strangely enough, listening is perhaps the most potent way we can affect another person's life.

It is impossible to overemphasize the immense need we humans have to be listened to, to be taken seriously, and to be understood. No one can develop freely in this world and have a fulfilling life without feeling understood by at least one person. Listen to all the conversations in our world between nations, as well as between couples. For the most part, they are "dialogues of the deaf." That is why a church without cells is not operating at its optimum — there is no one to listen to the members. All the time is spent listening to the pastor.

The most important thing we can do to solve a problem is understand it. Unfortunately, we never listen long enough to understand what the problem is, so we are never able to solve it. Instead of listening, we just take turns talking.

In order to listen effectively, postpone your desire to react, respond, or defend to what the other person is saying. The purpose of listening is to allow both of you to understand the situation more fully. Listening attentively will also make the other person feel special.

People need to feel this way in order to sense that they are loved. In fact, each of the following elements should be present in your cell group. Within the group, they should feel:

1. Safe
2. Defended
3. Supported
4. Belonging
5. Cared about
6. Accepted
7. Special

Everyone wants to be loved, and I believe nothing makes people feel supported, cared about, and special more than listening to them. Active listening is responsive, attentive, and considerate. It means listening with your eyes as well as with your ears. When you truly listen to someone, you give that person the freedom to explore at deeper levels who he is and where the real problem lies.

Again, love is best demonstrated by attentive listening. The leader's number-one job is to listen to his disciples. Only once the leader has heard will he be equipped and qualified to teach.

DESIGN CREATIVE QUESTIONS

We can cultivate our listening ability by designing and asking appropriate questions. Here are some sample questions we could ask in our cell meeting:

• What dreams have you thrown away or kept secret either because no one encouraged you to try it or because you feared you would fail?
• If you could do anything in the world and be certain of your success, what would it be?

- In what three specific ways could you improve your everyday communication?
- Where are you strong in communicating? Where do you hit snags?

These types of questions are called "ice-breakers." These questions inspire some people to start talking and others to start listening. The list of good questions is endless. Suffice it to say here that we need to ask questions that will deepen our relationships; therefore, truly effective questions are those in which both people discover something about themselves.

Seven Steps To Overcoming Relational Problems in the Cell

1. Accept ownership of the problem. If you care about the relationship but you believe the other person is at fault, it is still your problem. Accept ownership of it. Once you do, you will be willing to commit your time and energies to solving it.

2. Analyze the problem. Take the problem apart and identify its various components. This could require untangling numerous problems so you can focus on them one at a time. Decide whether this is a good time to ask "dumb questions" to challenge your assumptions. Keep a broad perspective, and avoid becoming emotionally hooked.

3. Define the problem in the best terms you know. Develop a workable definition that all parties can agree to and then write it down. It is critical to separate the symptoms from the real cause of the problem. Remember, the flipside of criticism is idealism. If someone is struggling with being too cynical, that's merely the symptom. They need to wrestle with the actual problem, which is their hidden idealism.

In other words, don't try to help the person become less cynical; help him to be more realistic. *That* is working on the core of the problem. Also, anger and apathy are expressions of frustration. Frustration begets anger, and anger begets apathy. Therefore, instead of reacting to anger or apathy, listen to the person's frustration.

4. Brainstorm. What are all the possible solutions that could be employed at this time? Anytime you can make finding the solution fun, you will improve not only the quantity of ideas, but the quality as well.

Take this opportunity to listen intently to others. Remember, sometimes you have to take the risk of making outrageous suggestions. If you want change, you must be willing to think sideways, backwards, around corners, and upside down. Limiting yourself to your regular patterns of thinking restricts you to seeing what you've always seen. This leaves little opportunity for change or problem solving.

5. Select a course of action to which everyone involved can commit. It is important to be able to clearly articulate why you believe this is the best selection. If you will clearly describe why this is the best plan, you will be much less likely to abandon it when the way becomes difficult.

6. Implement. You've planned your work — now work your plan. Work lovingly, for there is great joy in a well-built relationship. Remember to tap into the resources of the Master by bathing your work in prayer.

7. Evaluate. This is another chance to learn from your problem, even if you weren't successful in solving it. What you learn and how you learn it will allow you to move into deeper levels of mutual understanding and appreciation.

Relational problems are process-oriented. We will always be "in process," but some of these techniques will enable you to gain a greater definition of your problem so you can find loving, healthy solutions. However, not all these techniques are recommended for the cell group setting. Some of the processes given here for problem-solving are best implemented privately between the parties involved. Remember, of course, that singles of opposite sexes need to bring a friend along.

Stay Cool

Never forget — *the key to any great relationship is attentive listening.* Of course, in the heat of conflict, it is easy to forget the goals of your relationship. Wanting to be right is easier than wanting to understand the other person. These principles of relational problem-solving won't help you build defenses, but they *will* help you attack the problem and not the person.

You cannot afford to neglect the incredible power of love. Remember that God is love and that he who dwells in love, dwells in God and God in him (1 John 4:16). This love makes us fearless, and where there is no fear, there is true understanding.

The power of God's love will never be contained or understood. It is available to all and can literally produce miracles in relationships. Love is by far more important than anything else. It casts out fear. It covers a multitude of sin. It is absolutely invincible.

There is no difficulty that enough love will not conquer. There is no disease that enough love cannot heal; no door that enough love will not open; no gulf that enough love will not bridge. There is no wall that enough love will not throw down; no sin that enough love will not redeem. It makes no difference how dire the trouble, or how hopeless the outlook, or how great the mistake — love will dissolve it all!

I believe that when we put God in the center of our relationships, He can transform them. He empowers us to influence each other's lives because He is love.

The ultimate reason, then, for the cell group is to better express the love of God, not to have a bigger church. A cell setting expresses the love of God better than does a church setting because it provides more than an opportunity for people to hear — it provides a forum for them to be heard.

It's Time To Jump In!

As we have seen, the model of 12 enables a church to supernaturally fulfill the Great Commission, as called forth by Christ on the day of His ascent (Acts 1:8). This vision provides an opportunity for a local body of believers to achieve all they can be in Christ and to share the same language and purpose that is in the heart of the Father. Inherent within the model of 12 is a divine call in which all have the opportunity to excel.

Your church can be an instrument in global salvation! The G-12 cell church concept brings this proposal to you, for it is a vision without frontiers. It fits into any ministry that has a vision for growth and multiplication.

Therefore, I urge you to grasp this powerful vision and make the Kingdom of Jesus Christ grow until He comes back. Remember, you are called to change the reality of your city and to influence lives of others for Christ. My desire is to see the cloud of revival hovering over the entire world, and the G-12 system is a vital key to seeing that vision come to pass!

Perhaps your heart has been crying out for a way to help your church "jump in the river" and be an integral part of the Holy Spirit's mighty flow of power and glory in these last days. So my question to you is this: *What are you waiting for?* It's time to jump in and watch your church grow!

About The Author

Rocky Malloy is founder and president of *Shield of Faith Ministries, Inc.*, a mission's agency that administers missionary activities in Asia, Europe, North Africa and South America. He has administrative offices in The Netherlands, Bolivia, and the United States. *Shield of Faith Ministries* was founded in 1990 and has planted or assisted in planting churches in several countries around the world.

Rocky started his ministry in California after rededicating his life to Christ in December 1986. Since that time, he has preached the Gospel in many countries in Central and South America, as well as in Europe. A powerful and dynamic speaker, Rocky Malloy draws from his vast experiences as a sea captain, business owner, and building contractor to expound the Word of God. Rocky also has a motivating testimony of how God has saved him from several life threatening situations while serving in various countries.

In 1993, Rocky signed a contract with the Cuban government giving *Shield of Faith Ministries, Inc.*, authority to establish religious offices of human development (churches) in that country.

Rocky and his wife Joske pastor a G-12 cell church called *Iglesia Río de Vida (River of Life Church)* in Santa Cruz, Bolivia. The success of their G-12 church has given them the privilege of helping other pastors who desire greater success in their ministries. Rocky's earlier manuals about the G-12 cell system are already in use in more than 16 countries.

The Malloys also direct *Victory Bible Institute — Santa Cruz*, an affiliate of Victory Christian Center in Tulsa, Oklahoma. They implemented an extremely successful program in the Bolivian public school system, using Bible school students as volunteer teachers for Religion and Social Studies. At the time of this publication, thousands of public school students — using completely rewritten, Christian curriculum — are under the care of the volunteer Bible students. Other works of the church include a street ministry for children, rural evangelism, children's crusades, and economic development projects. Rocky and Joske have written various Bible school curricula that are being used in several Latin American countries.

The Malloys worked for four years on the border of Honduras and Nicaragua during the war between the Sandinistas and the Contras. They worked one year in the war zone and then for three years after the war on the Mosquito Coast of Honduras, helping to repatriate the refugees.

From 1987 to 1989, Rocky served in San Diego, California, at Horizon Christian Fellowship, then a cell church of 6,000. He also taught Missions, End Times, Spiritual Authority, Church History, and Cults in La Marque, Texas, at the Abundant Life School of Ministry Bible Institute. At one time, Rocky was also the editor-in-chief of *Ambassador*, a world news magazine written from a missions perspective. He also owned *Spirit Travel*, a travel agency for missionaries.

Rocky's wife, Joske, who is a Dutch citizen, was born and raised in the mission field of Indonesia. She lived the first 14 years of her life with Stone Age natives. Her parents are pastors/missionaries, and she has been active in the ministry her entire adult life. Rocky and Joske live in Bolivia with their four children: Ziza Zoe, Tabitha Ann, Roxann Luz, and Jerome Michael.

The Malloys invite you to partner with them and with *Shield of Faith Ministries* in all their endeavors. Pastor Rocky travels outside Bolivia, often helping churches capture the G-12 vision. If you would like assistance with the G-12 vision in your church, or if you would enjoy giving financial support to *Shield of Faith Ministries*, you may contact Rocky and Joske Malloy at the address on the following page.

For Further Information

To obtain additional copies of this book,
or to inquire about volume discounts,
contact the author at his United States office address:

P.O. Box 327
Texas City, Texas 77590

Voice-mail: 888.241.9185

E-mail: sofministries@hotmail.com